LAUNCH LIKE A ROCKET

Build the Soft Skills You Need
for Your Career
by Leveraging Your Entire College Experience

By Susan E. Lyon

This book is designed to provide accurate and authoritative information in regard to the subject matter covered. It is sold with the understanding that the publisher is not engaged in rendering legal, accounting, or other professional services. If legal or other expert assistance is required, the services of a competent professional should be sought.

Published by Lyon & Associates Creative Services, Inc.
3366 North Torrey Pines Court, Suite 110
La Jolla, CA 92037
LaunchLikeARocket.com

ISBN: 978-0-692-77629-2
Library of Congress Control Number: 2016915755

Library of Congress Cataloging-in-Publications Data
Lyon, Susan E.
Launch Like a Rocket: Build the Soft Skills You Need for Your
Career by Leveraging Your Entire College Experience
p.   cm.
Includes source references
ISBN: 978-0-692-77629-2
1. Business/Economics 2. Careers 3. College

Cover design: Jessica Gheen, nestwestdesign.com
Interior design: Mark Lyon, lyonassoc.com

10 9 8 7 6 5 4 3 2 1

First Edition
Printed in the United States

For my parents,
who gave me a lot of great advice,
and my sons,
who really are quite tired
of hearing my helpful tips.

CONTENTS

INTRODUCTION

This book and my blog are titled *Launch Like A Rocket*, because I think new college grads are a lot like shiny, beautiful, expensive new rockets. Out on the launchpad, what really powers a tall, shiny rocket into space so it can complete the planned orbit, are the booster rockets that help it break free. Yet we don't picture those in our mental image of a space launch. Just because those boosters get jettisoned as a rocket breaks free of earth's gravitational pull doesn't mean a tremendous amount of time and attention didn't go into developing the boosters. Without them, a rocket is just a very expensive object that can't accomplish any of its planned objectives. A college degree, no matter how shiny the GPA, major, or the issuing institution, isn't of much value without the soft skills to boost it into orbit.

Making Sure College Leads to Career Success

It seems like college admissions insanity hits a new high every single year. This mindset inevitably makes college admissions a finish line for many talented students. The storyline seems to go: Once in at Amazing U, pixie dust will be sprinkled and in four years your degree will make you magically employable for life. While it is true that some professions recruit heavily from particular schools (e.g., Wall Street firms from the Ivy League), studies show where you earn an undergraduate degree has almost no bearing on the future success of most students. The one exception is for disadvantaged students—they come to the table with a weak network via family and friends and a name-brand school can hook them up very effectively. If a student finishes high school certain they've already won the lottery and the school feels they've handed out the prizes, how can either side have any interest in what happens in the next four years? Students take the right classes to graduate with a degree in something valuable, hopefully in four years, and schools happily cash the students' (or their families') checks.

But what if college is a starting line? What if, once accepted, you stop and consider exactly what you want out of the next four years? Not just in class, because most students don't select or even start college with a major in mind, but what other things about a school attract you? What opportunities does the school provide outside the classroom? And what things do you want to be sure to accomplish? Once you graduate you're going to need to distinguish yourself from the pack, whether for graduate school or employment. Too frequently even students and parents who do think they are seriously considering the post-college world are counting on happy stories about the power of the sport, fraternity/sorority, or alumni network of a given program to yield these magical results. While those stories have a grounding in truth, no employment network can possibly absorb all the Alpha Phi sisters, Sigma Chi brothers, lacrosse players, or Urban and Regional Development majors who graduate in a given year from a given school. Even within these sometimes quite supportive and powerful networks, there is a sorting of qualifications, so it's important to work hard to be the most competitive candidate even with this kind of network advantage.

After reading Elizabeth Armstrong's and Laura Hamilton's book, *Paying for the Party: How College Maintains Inequality*, I'm further convinced that a side benefit of this kind of careful consideration will keep you out of narrow, inappropriate majors that rarely lead to the careers they appear to promise. Instead, you'll be making the kind of smart moves that naturally build a résumé that will give you a shot at the jobs you're interested in pursuing after graduation. It's likely that the job market will make big shifts, even in the four years you're in college. Add to that the strong probability that you will change a lot yourself, and there's really no knowing now exactly what opportunities will be both open and accessible to you. It's what you do in college outside the classroom that will open doors, create opportunities, and give you the soft skills that naturally make you one of the "lucky" ones all through your career.

The reality is that there is no way to predict the future any longer—no way to say which careers will be safe and stable for the entire length of your working life. Even doctors and lawyers are beginning to see their career paths alter as the world changes. The career ladder that once existed, whether within one company or through a series within an industry is largely gone. Sheryl Sandberg's book, *Lean In*, presented an alternative to the ladder metaphor in which a career path can be seen as a jungle gym. Most play structures are composed of equispaced rungs or triangles and are a stable, unswaying, fixed grid.

I think that a more organic structure is a better metaphor for your working career. If you picture a pond full of lily pads, the leaves appear in spreading clumps, with old ones decaying and disappearing while new growth appears in new places within the pond. If you're a frog living in that pond, you have to successfully navigate the pond's changing landscape. You jump from pad to pad, and the appealing new pads you want to jump over to need to be within your individual jumping range, wide and strong enough to sustain your landing force, and unpopulated enough to accommodate a new guy. While you're happy on one pad, the reality is that it's started to decay and new ones are blooming elsewhere as they begin their lifespans. Your career will also require that you leap from one opportunity to the next, sometimes because you've decided you need a change, sometimes because your employer has decided. You need to use these early years in college and right after graduation to position yourself to successfully navigate the jumps as they are required. Meanwhile industries, technologies, consumer tastes, and larger economic drivers will create and destroy opportunities all over the world. It's impossible to chart a path today precisely because half the rungs you plan on utilizing in the future won't be there or will be undesirable by the time you got to that stage. You need to learn from the start of your career to keep your eyes on the next step or two while working to excel at your current position, ensuring you've got the track record, the network, and the skills to make moves to a variety of alternate opportunities.

This should be an exciting prospect. The world today moves fast with new industries and technologies creating new opportunities. Your career never has to be boring, and all the skills you've mastered won't go to waste—you'll just keep an eye out to see how they might be redeployed in a new setting. Most people want to make the moves they make in their careers. They want more money, more responsibilities, something new, to change locations for better weather, to be closer to family, to more affordable housing, to accommodate a partner's next big opportunity. You will continue to change as you live your life, constantly finding new interests, so if you change, or life changes, and a move is desirable, you always have a number of choices. Sometimes industries do disappear. We don't see buggy whip manufacturers or telegraph operators in much demand today, but in the heyday of those careers, people didn't see computer programmers, drone operators, or data analysts as career options. A little regular maintenance will make it easy to avoid a massive, overwhelming undertaking at a time (like senior year) when you feel much more worried about the feasibility of your next move.

Regular work all through college with an eye to the longer-term future will make your senior year job hunt much more likely to yield a successful result. If your path involves a graduate degree, you'll have a strong competitive edge in those evaluations as well. The people who instinctively seek out chances to develop new skills, who are willing to consider new opportunities, reconsider established perspectives, and keep their networks well-tended, consistently reap the benefits throughout their careers. Their businesses survive downturns, they are quickly promoted to new positions, they move to new companies with increasing responsibilities. And they do all of these things a little faster than everyone else. While promotions and the accompanying raises are the hallmarks of the accepted definition of success for many prior generations, increasingly people view success through a more personal lens, seeking work that is interesting and personally meaningful. The financial rewards of successful people come out of that foundation. The key reason to work very hard to find the right path for you is because it won't feel like work. It will just make you happy and fulfilled. Once you've got that kind of meaningful employment, you'll want to keep finding it, whatever the economic cycle or the stage of your life.

If you are working your way through school, your free time will be in shorter supply, so choose those sustenance jobs wisely. Working as a nanny is always popular with college students, but most of the time it's a dead end—no networking, no contacts, no professional skill development. Even if you want to teach, it would be better to be working in a school or a Boys & Girls Club, managing groups of children in an educational setting. If you want to be a barista at Starbucks, think about the location. A few years part-time at the right Starbucks location and you could have some great career contacts as long as you're making an effort to chat up the regulars as time permits. Working will limit your ability to take on extracurricular activities to build supplemental skills, so it's even more important to choose your social activities wisely.

Studies show that salary inequalities start fast. Students who graduate in a bad economy tend never to catch up on salaries and spending two years in a dud job while someone else is getting promoted every year can also make a big difference. To the extent you can make your first jobs major successes and move quickly up the ranks, you will set expectations. Future managers will see that early track record and expect that you are a go-getter, who deserves increasing responsibilities and challenges. The more you learn, the more value you bring to the table, and the more opportunities you will see presented. If you are a rising star early on that creates unconscious bias in your favor, which can become a self-fulfilling prophecy as your career plays out.

Employer Needs

Employers are all over the web talking about the stunning lack of soft skills of new college graduates. In 2013, Martha C. White, writing for Time, noted "The annual global Talent Shortage Survey from ManpowerGroup finds that nearly 1 in 5 employers worldwide can't fill positions because they can't find people with soft skills. Specifically, companies say candidates are lacking in motivation, interpersonal skills, appearance, punctuality and flexibility." A January 2015 article in the Wall Street Journal discussed the results from the annual Collegiate Learning Assessment Plus test which showed 40% of the test-takers were less than proficient in the complex reasoning skills required of professionals. Journalist Douglas Belkin quoted Debra Humphreys, vice president for policy and public engagement of the American Association Colleges and Universities, saying "Employers are saying 'I don't care about all the knowledge you learned because it's going to be out of date two minutes after you graduate ... I care about whether you can continue to learn over time and solve complex problems.'" This lack of skills keeps small businesses from considering new grads at all and large ones not excited about the majority of their new hires. While employers may be willing to train you in their specific processes, if you can't handle the untrainable tasks, they can't set you loose in the work environment. In reporting on the results of a survey conducted by Marketplace.org and the Chronicle of Higher Education, reporter Amy Scott wrote of employer responses, "More than half of them said they have trouble finding qualified people for job openings. They said recent grads too often don't know how to communicate effectively. And they have trouble adapting, problem solving and making decisions—things employers say they should have learned in college."

This is why new graduates are so frustrated by most of the ads they see asking for a few years of experience. It's impossible to get experience if every job requires you already have a couple of years. If you spend four years completing classes, taking irrelevant jobs for the cash, and making the most of the college social scene, then you won't have any experience. And sure, you can try and get some internships to beef up your résumé, but how do you make yourself the most competitive candidate for those few openings?

Careers are built out of individual jobs, one after another, at the same company or different ones. The bottom line for any job is going to be whether you are worth your cost. The people worth their costs don't just tackle their list in order, one thing after another, even at top quality. But that *is* what A students do in a semester-long class. That's the disconnect right there.

Jobs are much more like writing a senior thesis—you have to synthesize those tasks into a cohesive narrative. Why are these things necessary? How do they fit together? What's the larger story? How do you fit into the organization's larger strategic plan? You need to see these things and knock through that to-do list with an eye to the larger objective. Only then will you be valuable.

It's actually pretty easy to be a standout when the competition isn't playing to win. College environments provide a wide array of terrific opportunities to work for free, letting you pick and choose how you spend your time, creating a great profile, and making sure you can confidently apply for jobs that ask for experience, knowing you do have experience. If you've been selling advertising for the school's alumni magazine or calling parents for donations while earning your degree, you do have experience, even if it has been part-time. You can apply for those jobs with a great cover letter making your case, even if your degree is brand-new. Sometimes you have to do the work for free to show that you're good enough to be paid. Whether you're a student, a parent, or a college, I'm proposing that a few minor adjustments can make it possible for a student to graduate with all the skills they need at the same time they are meeting the academic requirements to graduate.

In college you major in a subject (or two). Some schools have professional degrees such as Advertising, Graphic Design, Computer Science, or Petroleum Engineering. Their grads in those majors should have completed a curriculum that gives them concrete skills in marketing, typography, coding languages, or geology. This should makes them employable if they can find a match. Also, some fields are desperate for new grads (if you get your timing right). As I write this, the smart students who studied petroleum engineering are graduating into a great economy that is terrible for the oil industry. What's important to note is that no matter how in-demand your skills are when you start your major or graduate, the world keeps changing. Soft skills let you keep moving and changing with it, to new fields and new industries.

Some colleges have majors like English, Philosophy, or Physics. The grads in those fields can write, analyze arguments, or solve problems. In a traditional liberal arts school, all three of those majors will be able to do all three of those things and a lot more. They have a head start on soft skills, but even those students still need a lot of practice implementing their skills in the real world. All students, at all schools, in all majors, need a huge amount of help packaging their college experience into an employable profile. Even if one of my sons was going to graduate and come work for our business right after graduation, they'd have a paycheck, but they'd have to work even harder to make a case to clients, vendors, and coworkers that they deserved any respect at all. No one gets free ride on packaging themselves after graduation.

Okay, so now for the big question: what are soft skills? Businesses have a lot of phrases to describe their ideal candidates, some of which are obvious, while others require a little more explanation. They look for grads who can solve complex problems (adapting and integrating ideas), taking the abstract to the concrete, overcome obstacles, cope under pressure, collaborate, communicate, prioritize and organize, manage projects, work in teams, and learn over time. They expect interview skills, some business sense, and would like to see some creativity because creative thinking leads to the best problem solving.

Most of these skills are not built into the American educational system. If you're lucky, your academics will have provided some chances to work on team projects. Some readers will already have these skills. Extroverts tend to have some advantages in outbound communication, although typically that leads to weaknesses with inbound communication. The passionate community activist will have be motivated to tackle projects and make things happen, picking up skills along the way.

In the interest of making this book full of actionable information, I've broken the soft skills into four major groups: Communicate, Organize, Relate, and Execute (CORE). Within those four CORE groups, I've listed the smaller subsets of those skills. Communicate breaks into Write and Speak; Organize breaks out into People, Time, and Money; Relate breaks into Groups and Diversity; while Execute breaks out into Follow-through, Results, and Long-range Planning.

Within these subsets I explain the ways they are used in the business world and provide tactical suggestions for groups and activities that will permit you to get those experiences while you're working on your degree. Each college is a unique place, and they are ever-changing over the years. They, too, have to adapt to a changing world or face extinction. The schools and programs that I highlight are examples of the kinds of things every campus offers. But in any instance, I would hope you would adapt the ideas to your interests and passions. Anything that can be done for the newspaper can also be done for the campus Democrats, your sorority, the black students association, or campus service group.

My Vantage Point

I co-founded an advertising agency more than 25 years ago. Our clients are in the technology, biotech, health, and finance industries. In the last 10 years we've moved to focusing exclusively on film production and added other creative firms to our client list. As the mother of two sons, one halfway through his undergraduate degree, one in graduate school, I've always made a point of being willing to do informational interviews with college students and recent grads.

My sons chose small liberal arts colleges from the book *Colleges That Change Lives.* My oldest son, Nick, graduated (in four years) from the University of Puget Sound in Tacoma, Washington, majoring in biology and minoring in the humanities, with a concentration in bioethics. Our younger son, Jake, is a junior at Denison University in Granville, Ohio (outside Columbus), majoring in philosophy and economics. I currently serve on the Denison Parent Advancement Council and served for four years on the University of Puget Sound Parent Council.

What I came to realize in talking to so many college students and young professionals, is that there's a gap between a college's expertise in educating a student and what the career world is requiring. Despite a concerted, successful effort in creating student opportunities for internships, externships, informational interviews with alumni and parents, there's little discussion to enable students to understand the required soft skills conceptually, much less a training process to ensure they build, deploy, and improve those skills. While many colleges have strong career development offices, it's up to the student to show up and avail themselves of those services. Too many students show up after the winter break of senior year, scrambling to figure out what's next.

There's almost a language barrier, despite the best efforts of very good career placement offices. I believe that college is the last chance to think big, impractical ideas, to look at subjects you may never encounter again, and that there's a great reason for a liberal arts education—looking at a cross-section of the world's knowledge while you find your passion. I don't suggest colleges and universities should be teaching trades, but I do think that we've got to find a way to bridge that gap if we want the best ideas out of the brightest minds, we as a society, are graduating, and if those graduates want satisfying, re-warding careers that last a lifetime through all kinds of changes.

I also realized that the same massive load of extracurriculars that gets great teenagers into college continues all through college. And those extracurriculars are perfectly suited to fill the gap. They are real-world environments, with all the same messy issues that come up in my clients' companies and in my own small business. Plus, they are open to anybody, so if you're missing a skill set, you can jump in and get it. The stakes aren't high, so inexperience is welcomed, and that freedom to tackle something for which you have little or no qualification is something most people will never encounter again. You're free to dabble, make shorter-term commitments, and learn from your peers and your mistakes. In *Aspiring Adults Adrift*, Richard Arum and Josipa Roksa call out that in their research "Students noted how engagement in clubs and campus organizations helped broaden their horizons." Unfortunately, they also go on to note that "Getting along with others...may often mean getting along with similar others," which doesn't help in a world that requires lots of working with dissimilar others to yield the best products, processes, and results.

It's a little easier to build from the right foundation, which is why the ideal scenario would be to give serious thought to these kinds of things while you're choosing a college. For example, Puget Sound was on our older son's college list because they have a strong, funded summer research program. For a student like Nick, who was inter-ested in graduate school in science, that looked like a key advantage. Even for a Biology major who wants to go straight to work, it's un-usual for large numbers of undergraduates at big research univer-sities to have enough access to master using all the lab equipment. If you're interested in the sciences, this is the kind of activity that needs to be on your list of skills to acquire in the next four years, so be careful to confirm that the school you are picking can provide those kinds of opportunities. You may want to wait and add the big-name research university to your résumé for graduate school—you need an undergraduate education that sets you up for the next big goal you want to tackle. But if you're already at a big school with a doctoral program, and competing against grad students for access, you can develop an unwillingness to take no for an answer and get into a lab. (And an ability to gracefully make your case until you get the result you need is a really valuable soft skill.) Even quiet observation while cleaning out lab supplies is a small step forward. And a few conversations with those grad students can yield good advice, and possibly give you a fast start to building a relevant professional network. Make lemonade if your choice has turned out to be more of a lemon than you expected. And if the situation can't be fixed, then do look at transferring. Once the clock starts ticking and the money starts burning, transferring can feel like a mistake, but the reality is that life is full of zigs and zags and false starts that require a little backtracking so you end up at the destination you wanted, are a fact of life.

In my conversations, I kept thinking there must be a book that covers all of this advice for students that I could recommend, but when I started digging I found that most books are focused on getting into college or on getting a job. It appears as though everyone is content to ignore four years of college. Given how much thought and effort goes into college admissions, maybe students and their parents are just too tired to think about the next big project. I suspect students don't see how short those four years are and parents are either moving their focus onto the next kid in the queue or getting used to their newly empty nest. Since I have an empty nest and some newly opened up free time, I figured I'd write the book I wanted to recommend to all the students I spoke with and maybe extend my reach a little further into the world.

Throughout, I've tried to flag the shortcomings of some venues you might feel are nicely addressing a given issue. While the skills sections might be interesting to parents and other stakeholders, they are directed towards what students themselves can do in the course of being involved in their new community. Everything I suggest simply requires that you get involved as more than a participant in your extracurricular life at college. Nothing should cost much additional money and the examples are only examples. You should be working for things that are relevant to you—groups and activities you'd like to see continue to thrive at your college. The only requirement to implement these ideas is to slowly, consistently push yourself out of your comfort zone, until that zone is very large. The goal is for you to be able to honestly believe that you do have the skills and experience to apply for and successfully win the jobs that look appealing to you as college comes to an end. I want you to have the experiences it takes to write a cover letter explaining why you're a great fit for a given job, a résumé and LinkedIn profile that get you the interviews you want, and a wide range of relevant examples you can draw on in those interviews to show why you'd be an ideal candidate for the position. There's a big difference between just telling someone you're a great organizer/budgeter/writer and being able to give two examples of instances where you demonstrated skills in a real-world situation.

I've also included smaller sections at the end to outline some ideas about what parents and colleges can do to better facilitate students gaining the relevant skills. Finally, at the very end of the book, I include an appendix that covers the basics of making a professional impression. While it's likely too remedial for most college students, it may be useful to high school students beginning to visit colleges and interview with admissions officers and local alumni.

COMMUNICATE

The Chronicle of Higher Education's 2012 study noted most employers were reporting "recent grads too often don't know how to communicate effectively". In talking about the concept for Launch Like A Rocket with my professional network, the feedback I received again and again was that intern and new graduate communication skills were weak or even unprofessional. Unprofessional is a disaster—that's the difference between internships turning into job offers and first jobs not turning into first firings. And the thing about "unprofessional" criticisms is that many employers aren't going to discuss it with you. It's viewed as unfixable and undiscussable. Ultimately great leaders are strong listeners. If you think you're already great in front of a crowd, be sure that you're also really listening, not just waiting to talk. You're not always going to know exactly why that internship or job didn't work out the way you had hoped when the shortcoming is in your communication skills. I'm pretty sure your parents, coaches, and professors have covered a lot of the basics involved in making a good impression, so I'll skip discussing the unspoken signals you are sending out. I have a few specifics in the appendix, if you want a quick review.

What I see time and time again, at all stages of schooling, is that good communicators win opportunities for themselves, and those public successes raise their profile, yielding more opportunities for both practice and more success. In the work world, it works much the same way. Junior staff with strong spoken or written skills get to present or create the proposals that move the business forward, and helping to win those accolades, grants, or accounts puts you on the fast track for more managerial responsibilities. Successes like that are also clear evidence of your value to your employer, so they give you a chance in a review to ask for more money, whether in bonuses, raises, or promotions. As those opportunities raise your profile within your organization, you build a network and a reputation that leads to new opportunities outside the company. For any of that to happen you've got to be visible, and the difference between two equally good technical people will boil down to those skills, whether the technical skill is as a chef, a programmer, an editor, or a new associate.

WRITTEN COMMUNICATIONS

Writing is a big part of all professions at some level. And it's not a skill that ever stops being needed. You're always going to write cover letters, emails, résumés, thank you notes, blog comments (if not your own blog), LinkedIn profile updates, or whatever comes along to replace those things over time. The more you write, the better you get. It would be nice to think that college courses are going to handle this for you, but in Richard Arum's and Josipa Roksa's *Aspiring Adults Adrift,* they note that their research for their earlier *Academically Adrift* showed "Fifty percent of (sophomore) students had no single class which required more than 20 pages of writing." This may raise some concerns at your chosen school with your chosen major, but that's why electives exist, and why, GPA considerations aside, it's worth going outside of your comfort zone when choosing those electives, particularly in your first two years. To get both a lot of practice writing and consistent, good-quality feedback so you can improve, you've got to take some classes with those kinds of assignments.

If your academic track alone is giving you a lot of practice, it may not be exactly the right kind of writing. In Daniel F. Chambliss' and Christopher G. Takacs' *How College Works*, they write, "Professors differ in the kinds of arguments they allow, the kind of logic and evidence they expect, and in the tone of the writing they encourage." Academic writing is much different from the writing you encounter in the business world, just as that, in turn, is very different from the writing of grant proposals. In reading background material as research for this book, I had many forceful reminders of the variety of styles out there. Academic writing may be a career advancement requirement for scientists and professors, but those few academics who can also write popular books develop a supplemental income and raise their profile, thereby enhancing their university's image. And while writing may not be a requirement for many careers, with the advent of self-published editorial content on platforms like LinkedIn, those who can write well have an ability to establish themselves as subject matter experts. Best of all, those kinds of opportunities are self-created. You're not stuck waiting for your company to notice you and give you a forum, and you may not have to contact the competition in search of a new position—instead people will organically notice and reach out to you.

Write Proposals

On some level everything you touch in the working world is a proposal. You're proposing they hire you, then proposing clients hire your employer or buy your employer's product or fund your grant. You're potentially freelancing on the side, proposing a landlord take you as a tenant, that people date you, have coffee with you, invite you to their book club/party/bowling team. So you've done a lot of this your whole life, and some of it has been in writing. There is a tendency in college to go ask in person, probably because you need some guidance to this new community's processes. I think this is probably a holdover from being a child at home and a minor in high school: You needed to ask permission. But a proposal isn't asking permission. You're making the case for something to happen, whether it's a new event on campus or asking for a class to be counted towards an elective degree requirement.

One of the things I love about small liberal arts colleges is that many have summer research programs. Whether you end up doing research or not, writing a formal proposal that goes through a committee review is incredibly valuable. Make sure you get feedback, whatever the result. Not only should you be getting feedback from an advisor before you submit, but whether funded or not, draft a short note to the committee, thanking them, and asking if they have any feedback on how your proposal could be improved. The great thing about college is that everyone employed on that campus is (or should be) really interested in helping you grow. You may encounter people who are too busy at a given moment in time, but don't be shy about asking for feedback. If the answer is, "I am just jammed this week with finals coming up," let them know you'd love to have a brief call or meeting after finals are over. Or perhaps they can jot down some quick notes via email over the break. Yes, they'll be inundated if everyone asks, but my larger point in this book is that no one else is asking.

No matter how large or small the school, you're bound to find there's something you're interested in that doesn't exist. Alternatively, you may find that there is a rule or tradition or group on campus that really shouldn't exist. Whether you think there should be a new major, a new sport, a new organic co-op garden, a program to mentor local high school students, or that your school should add family or transgender bathrooms, change the mascot, or abolish the Greek system, the next step is to find out who has some decision-making ability in this arena. While you undoubtedly have a clear argument for your point of view, you need to discover something about that potential audience and their preferences to determine the best way to structure your proposal.

Even if you determine that the way forward is a public rally or protest, you're going to need to write out your proposal in supporting op-eds for the student and/or local paper, in blog posts, and other media. Depending on the scale of your proposed change, you may need to convert others to your cause, and once they join up, you need to be sure you're speaking with one voice. The only way to get there is to have a written proposal or foundational document that outlines the current state of affairs, the problem that poses, the proposed change(s), and an action plan to accomplish your desired outcome. No matter how clear all these things are, even if your audience is predisposed philosophically to grant your proposal, a proposal that doesn't have a plan to cover the financial implications leaves your audience with an easy way to say no. There's really no way to combat a rejection based purely on "we can't afford it." The process of writing a proposal, and thinking through all the counter arguments and objections, will strengthen your skills.

This is not like an ongoing argument with your parents, where you can endlessly come back with new arguments to rebut their new objections. You get one bite at the apple, so the presentation has to address everything. At the same time, the proposal has to be short enough to read in a reasonable amount of time. While you are incredibly vested in the idea, your audience is not, so you've got to make the time commitment approachable for them. Whether the process is simple or difficult, whether you accomplish your goals or not, this kind of experience is invaluable working in any organization.

Write Presentations

Classes should be requiring you speak in class, so you're practicing spoken presentation skills regularly, but look for classes or extra-curriculars that require a presentation. Even the best speakers will sometimes need to present their information visually and the world is already far too full of terrible PowerPoint presentations. There's a real skill to these and whole books have been written on the subject, but the more you can practice, the more you'll find what works for you with your strengths and weaknesses as a speaker. There are so many templates it's possible for a first-timer to do a fairly decent job of abiding by basic design principles so the presentation looks good. I also think presentations can be a great chance to work collaboratively with someone who is more visual and get their guidance on colors, icons, fonts, and use of space. After all, they need to practice their practical skills as well as their soft skills in client management, so it's a win on two fronts for them. Your audience will always be full of people who learn and retain information in different ways, so the strength of a presentation is to reach out to the more visual learners, while underlining key points for the auditory learners. And with every speaker competing against the smartphones in nearly every hand, anything you can do to keep your audience's eyes on you will help their ears and brains stay on you as well. Classes that require this kind of work will be graded, of course, but if they don't involve some kind of feedback from your peer audience, then be sure you seek out feedback from a few people in the class. You need to have a feel for a wide variety of viewpoints to be sure you're mastering the skills you're working to obtain.

If your classes are weak in this regard, any group with regular board meetings of more than a half dozen people can provide an opportunity to prepare and practice. The larger and more diverse the mindsets of your audience, the better. Most schools tend to have a variety of students represented through their Associated Student Body organization's board. Typically far less diverse, but also a larger group, would be the interfraternity or Panhellenic council. These types of organizations have regular meetings with organized agendas and rules, and that structure accommodates equally structured presentations for both new ideas and educational updates.

Do some research into what makes a good presentation! If you just refuse to do the prep for a presentation outside of classes, my one design tip is to keep in mind that the presentation the audience sees should not be the same things as the one you see. There are areas for speaker's notes for a good reason: If the audience can read your presentation in full on the screens you present, they will, but they'll do so by ceasing to listen to anything you are saying. A strong written presentation is one skill, while developing the matching, supporting visual presentation should yield a much more stripped down version—one that requires listening to your talk in order for the slides to make sense. Don't ever create a visual presentation that makes your participation obsolete.

Write Emails

Emails are a necessary evil in the real world. Whether the technology eventually gets replaced by collaboration tools like Slack, project organization tools like Evernote, or some other new tool, they all require some basic skill in writing effectively. What all these tools share is that the communication is meant to accomplish both a short-term objective such as setting a meeting or call or updating the facts, and also to serve as a long-term reference point as the project continues, if only for contact information. Your internship and job hunts will definitely require cover letters to yield personal interviews. Years of extremely short-form communication with people you already know have shortchanged this skill-building for most people.

My kids knew my career had trained me to both read and quickly respond to emails (I love to clear my inbox), so it was a great way to get me to consider information and make a fast decision—particularly in the middle of the work day. At age 12, our younger son, Jake, wanted an Airsoft gun, and knew I was opposed for several reasons. His strategy, knowing his audience so well, was to send me an email with his argument, understanding I'd consider it in a business mode and be inclined to issue a verdict quickly.

Jake's email read:

> First, let me describe to you what an Airsoft gun is. Airsoft guns are plastic devices that use compressed air to fire small, hollow, plastic pellets at targets (or people). They do not hurt at all. I have been shot before and it feels like a flick on the arm. I believe I should get one of these because I feel I am responsible enough not to shoot someone in the eye or anywhere on the face. Even if a stray shot hits me or any of my Airsoft-owning friends in the eye, it would ping off our shooting glasses.
>
> One issue many bring up is that these look very real and could cause some chaos, but the Airsoft gun I want to get is a brand called clearsoft. That means that most of the gun is made of clear plastic so anyone can see the springs inside and know it is not real. If I get an Airsoft gun, I won't be the kind of dumb ass that points it at a cop or anyone 'packing heat' and gets shot for real. This is why I believe that I should own this Airsoft gun. It is $45 and I will cover the cost of it in February when I can withdraw from my savings account or when you pay me at the end of the month for taking out the office trash.
>
> (A picture and link was attached.)

Keep in mind he was 12, writing to me as his mother, so he has a lot of leeway with the tone for both those reasons. (It does all depend on the person, of course. We have always had a pretty direct conversational style. My dad probably wouldn't have appreciated the tone had I written him similarly when I was 12.)

You've got to be able to write a similarly structured email to explain why you should get anything in business. Short, clearly requesting what you're looking for, dispensing with a perhaps obvious objection, and asking for a time to meet, to discuss further. Particularly smart in Jake's email is not to tell me he would also buy glasses and always wear them but to present a scenario where that was a given—"it would ping off our shooting glasses." That presentation makes the wearing of safety glasses a cultural given, making it easy for him to sidestep the argument around eye safety altogether. Jake was allowed to buy the Airsoft gun via return email.

Luckily, you've got a ton of opportunities to practice this in college. Take advantage of all chances to practice. Every time you need to send an email, consider whether it clearly states your proposal, is addressed to the right people, has a relevant subject line, and contains a signature with your non-email contact info. Send emails even if it's not required. Don't spam people, but practice. In addition to practicing emails, you're also practicing not doing the bare minimum. You're practicing thinking about what has to happen next to ensure the third and fourth things go smoothly.

If you arrange after class to meet with your professor or are planning to drop by during regularly scheduled office hours, email and confirm the convenience of the time and tell them what you're hoping to discuss and maybe how much of their time you're looking to consume. If you want to discuss changing majors, you may need an hour—and you may need other people in that meeting. Perhaps your current professor will realize that they should invite a colleague from the other department to help the meeting accomplish your goals and that it should be rescheduled as a result. (Read *The Thinking Student's Guide to College: 75 Tips for Getting a Better Education* by Andrew Roberts for some tips on other things professors would like to discuss.)

There are plenty of blog posts telling you what should be in an email, but the very basic requirements are a relevant subject (change it if you are responding to a thread that has taken a new turn) and a signature with your contact info. Yes, they have your email address, but many email addresses don't give away your actual name (please see the appendix on the basics for a section titled "Consider your Email Address"), and a phone number is always useful. There is a point at which any written dialogue needs to jump to an actual conversation. Any meeting can involve a last-minute change by one party, so the mobile number is key to the last-minute text update. The best possible outcome to an email proposal in business is that I pick up the phone and call you because I am so intrigued or committed to resolving the issue. Make it easy for me to move towards yes.

Send the email TO the person who needs to take action. COPY anyone else. If two people need to take action, then send it to both, but call out your expectations or hopes. An email sent to two people would read:

> "Susan, I'm hoping you can get me the street address-es for the local businesses that donated to our car wash for the animal shelter. I need them by Friday so I can drop by this Saturday and thank them all in person. Rachel, I do need all the photos by Thursday, so I have time to write the thank you notes Friday before I stop by."

Now Rachel and I both know what you need, why you need it, and by when. And we both know that you are relying on the two of us to deliver so you can execute something specific on a timeline. We are clear on the action, the deadline, and the reason. If we can't do it, we should be feeling some pressure to find a way to get it done, and we certainly should be picking up the phone to explain the prob-lem. If you get an auto-reply "out of town" email, you also know you need to reach out to someone else, or reschedule your plans. If it's not clear who should take the lead on a given item after a kick-off meeting or due to a vacation or illness, the best strategy is still to send it to one person and copy other possible options. This keeps the pressure on one person to either confirm they've got it handled or respond to all, with an answer as to who will be taking responsibility. Keep the email short. If 20 people have one sentence to-do items, then individually email them, or group them by interrelated tasks. Don't try my earlier email formula when assigning responsibilities to 20 recipients—some people may not read far enough down to see you've got something for them in the list. If you think a meeting is in order, I cover the value of building skills in running a meeting in the "Speaking" chapter.

To save yourself some of the more common operator-error email gaffes, add any attachments, write the body of the email, then write the subject line (sometimes you start out talking about one thing and then it turns out that's not a good summary), and only then add your recipients. This bottom-up building process saves you from sending unfinished emails that end mid-sentence, emails that lack the referenced attachment, or are not addressed to all the right people. It won't save you from sending it to the wrong Hannah or Joe when your mail program decides to auto complete the line, so always double-check the addresses before you hit send.

While we're talking about writing emails, there a few social niceties to replying to them as well. Most of the basic rules arise from the same central principle: don't waste anyone's time. Thus your reply, like any email, should have your basic signature with only relevant contact information. It is the rare person who wants your office fax number. And the rare business that still uses a fax that extensively. No one wants your company logo as a jpeg attachment, but it may be part of your corporate guidelines. Typically a group email will ask a set of people to all submit the same thing to the requester; their photo, their phone number, or what they can bring to the potluck. That email requires that you reply only to the requester, NOT to the whole group. Even emails that request possible meeting times are not an occasion for reply all, as the requester will be doing the coordination so only they need the information in your reply. Emails that are informational do not require a "thanks" or "no problem." Don't put anything in an email that would be a problem if forwarded to someone else other than the intended recipient.

If you're not going to be able to reply to an email request fairly quickly, then reply letting the person knowing what your timeline for getting back to them is: "I'm running out to a meeting, but will check with the team this afternoon and let you know before the close of business when we'll be getting you the next revision for your review." Better yet, be proactive with people and send an email letting them know what the schedule is before they ask, although always under-promise and over-deliver. In our business, we may think we're going to be able to turn around a set of revisions we receive on Tuesday morning by Thursday afternoon, but things do pop up or can turn out to be more difficult than anticipated. For example, when we receive revisions, we look over them quickly with the team, and a producer emails that we'll be sending a new link for review on Friday around lunch. If the client replies that they are taking a long weekend and leaving Thursday night, then we hustle to get it to them before the end of Thursday, likely updating them that morning that we are going to get it to them by early afternoon. Now they can plan their day to enable a new round of feedback before they leave. This helps them feel good about their weekend off, and helps us keep a project moving.

In using an email alternative like Slack to collaborate with a group, the rules are much the same. Your written messages should be clear and succinct, with all the information needed. Attachments should have sensible, searchable names. Assume everything will be read by everyone sooner or later, despite the ability to privately message, so watch what you say. And again, don't waste people's time. Things posted in the random channel should be somehow relevant to work—a great review of a new TV show that you know a lot of people have been considering watching is relevant, but unless you've got a cat video meme going, skip the cat videos. As with many things, you have to judge the culture and figure out what's appropriate. And think about how you look with all your postings in aggregate. Are you the funny animal video girl who clearly spends too much time on the Internet? Post a link to a book review or a new travel blog. I recommend everything in moderation as people form opinions based on the information you provide, so it's up to you to curate those offerings wisely.

SPOKEN COMMUNICATION

Speak in Meetings

Many of us in the work world are consumed by meetings. It's a huge part of getting things done, or NOT getting them done. Sure, your classes have "meetings" but this is a whole other beast. While you'll start your career as a listener, you should envision progressing in time to being an expert and a speaker on some scale. Being an expert doesn't magically happen eight years in the future. It happens because you get assigned a task and you make yourself expert in an arena, no matter how small. If you're approaching everything with a big-picture world view, you should be able to tackle a task and come away with some questions you want to clarify to fit it into the bigger picture, and then some insights into how it might be fine-tuned. Everyone with new, fresh eyes on an area has a potentially valuable, albeit brief, ability to provide insights. Once you are familiar with a system, you accept how it is being done, and you lose that window. Of course, be prepared to ask questions from a perspective of wanting to understand, not as a mere pretense to unleash your brilliant insights, that may actually result from an incomplete understanding. As an example of what fresh eyes bring to the table, after years as a chapter vice president of technology and two years as national webmaster for Teen Volunteers in Action, I knew the website inside and out. I was one of a small cadre of acknowledged TVIA web experts. Just as I was tidying up a few details before ending my decade of volunteer work with TVIA, our national president asked me to update the revised member requirements throughout the site. This entailed linking the one-page public site to a Google Drive document set to view only, and copying and pasting the same information to the appropriate Member Requirement pages in each of five chapter subsites. After carefully doing this work six times over, the president asked me if, when future changes were made, the information would self-populate to the chapter websites. Sadly, the answer was no. Because the five sub-sites each had a Member Requirement web page that they linked to from a side menu (not even in the main menu navigation), I had fixed the five pages because *we'd always had those five web pages.* The president's less technical view of the website map enabled her to back up and take the larger view. Of course, with that one logical question, it was apparent the five sub-pages should be deleted and the side menu link should be to the same view-only Google Drive-located document. It was a much more elegant and future-proofed solution, but I was just too close to the site to take that kind of worldview in making my one last update. You don't want to go out after 10 years of service with one bone-headed misjudgment. I was lucky to have a great partner in the work who could catch those things. Sometimes, the brilliant insight really requires a fresh look to spark a very real improvement.

Let's talk about business meetings and what you can get out of the different meeting genres. You want to maximize the value of your time in meetings once you are in the working world, as well as build skills for those meetings while you are still in college. Corporate meetings come in two main sizes, which impacts how you can interact, much as you are used to doing in classes with size differences. There are big meetings, when a large group shows up to be lectured at by someone at the front of the room. The speakers have information they think is vital to convey. By stopping all company work for their town hall, all hands meeting, or monthly webcast, they are signaling the seriousness of the matter at hand. It costs a lot of money to have everyone stop working at the same time. Pay attention. Just as a giant introductory class might not be the most interesting part of a given academic subject, it's foundational for everything that will come later. You still need to listen and make sure you're getting the material down. You're in no position to guess what's relevant and what's not. It's also a great chance to get a feel for the larger culture in any new job (or with any new client or vendor). How do the folks on stage dress? What do they look like? I'd take it to heart if I only saw really old white guys on the stage or you're in marketing but the only people ever on stage are the folks from finance and operations. There's a subtext you can read if you pay attention. Even if the spoken content isn't all that interesting, pay attention to everything else. And if you don't love the content, all the more reason to think about who is a good speaker and why. What lessons can you learn from how they get the rest of the audience to respond? Or fail to engage them? Is everyone around you looking rapt? Or checking their email on their phone? I admit some meetings are boring, and the content may actually be worthless to you at this stage, but those meetings can present opportunities to meet other people in the company. Sit next to new people and introduce yourself. Go with a goal to introduce yourself to certain people you think it would be great to take to coffee. That's a natural progression once you've met them, a great way to build a network, and maybe even find a mentor within your company.

There are small meetings, much like the seminars you've had in college. These are to discuss something and should lead to a clear set of action items for specific people in the room. Sometimes someone takes notes. Don't *volunteer* for this office housework if you are *already* invited to a meeting but suggesting you should be added to the invitee list to take notes—if you are good at taking notes—can give you access to a fantastic learning opportunity.) First off, be on time. Listen, but also talk when you've got something to contribute. If you have a question, probably someone else does, too. I think speaking in a meeting is a lot like a double Dutch jumping rope entrance—watch the rhythm, the earlier participants, get ready, double check your plan, and then, if it still seems right, go ahead and jump into the fray. Of course, there are meetings where your boss might take you just to observe, so in that case, don't talk in the meeting, but definitely ask privately for a debrief with your boss or someone else who might be able to help give context.

A good meeting has an agenda and someone running it—likely whoever asked for the meeting. A good one will end on time. Conference calls also count as meetings. If it doesn't end on time and is making you late for another meeting, politely let everyone know you have to go. If you go into a meeting knowing your time is tight, sit near the exit, and let everyone know at the start that you have a hard stop. Don't interrupt the meeting to leave. If you need to leave briefly for the restroom, then do so, but do so quietly. Ideally leave your stuff there, so it's clear you'll be back. Don't even look at your phone while in the meeting. Turn it off and put it away. Even taking notes on an electronic device is risky—people can't tell what you are doing. Typing even on an onscreen keyboard, makes noise, and you will be focused on the screen, getting no human subtext at all.

A great way to get practice running meetings is to start with your advisor. Ask for a meeting and come in with an agenda—not a secret agenda, a bullet-pointed one with your one to three goals for the meeting. It doesn't need to be written, but if you're going to refer to notes, provide copies. Make sure they know the agenda ahead of time, so they have any information or people that might also be required.

Form there, move on to group meetings. Take charge of something on campus, whether it's a fundraiser, a dinner, or a study group. You need to start figuring out how to control rambling TMI speeches and the one lonely human who just likes to hear themselves speak. In order to not be that person, try to limit your speaking time to your percentage of the table. If you have 10 people at the meeting, talk 10 percent of the time. Even if you are running a meeting, the best leaders want to hear discussion. (Leading is about getting the best out of your team, not about doing all the work yourself or micromanaging everyone else's efforts.) Go around the table and ask each relevant person for their opinion on the issue. (Unless the meeting is everyone reporting back–in that case, only the person who had the action item should speak to that issue.) Don't let side discussions, topical or between neighbors, derail the meeting (nicely suggest they go offline at another time and report back). If you have weak points in your performance, attend other meetings and watch the leaders for style when you don't need to be focused on content. Start your meetings saying you want to end on time and there's lots to cover...You can keep coming back to that theme, nicely cutting off the long-winded by saying, "That's a really interesting point, but I want to be mindful of the schedule, so let's move on to the next thing on the agenda." Summarize the meeting at the end with the action items agreed upon and the one person responsible for each item. Even if there's a team lining up sponsors for the animal shelter pet bath fundraiser, one person needs to be sure that team is on track and have ultimate responsibility to the larger group.

If you're really stumped for feedback on your skills, see if the adviser for your campus group, someone from career services, or someone from the philanthropic organization you're supporting can attend and give you feedback afterwards. (Ideally, you want to know they are good at meetings before asking.) Ask around to find out who is really good at running faculty or administrative meetings—it could turn out it's the executive chef for all the campus dining halls. If they don't seem to be giving you good feedback, tell them where you felt you didn't get the result you wanted—maybe they saw other ways you could have reached your goal. Most people work on campus in part because they actually like helping students. Get used to feeling a little awkward in an effort to make a connection. That's a whole other skill that's worth having. Most people will be flattered to be asked and, if they can't help you, they'll refer you to someone else who will.

Speak to a Large Audience

Colleges excel at providing opportunities for students to talk in front of large groups. You may not ever need this skill at work in a given career, but you will inevitably need it in life. As you develop expertise or discover a cause you feel passionately about, you will need to stand in front of a group of interested students, coworkers, a city council, or other civic group, and say your piece. Unfortunately, the skill of the presenter is a big part of what adds weight to the actual words being spoken, so bad ideas can win just because someone is an excellent speaker. I trust all your ideas will be great, so I encourage you to seek out these opportunities. You can join extracurricular groups focused on getting on a stage as part of a group, whether to act, sing, debate, or present. While many talented musicians have learned to be comfortable under observation when they are performing, speaking to the group is a different thing altogether. So simply be the student who introduces the pieces being performed or who does the opening welcome. Speaking in front of a group is much easier when you feel passionately about the message, so start with being passionate about the talents of your peers, performing someone else's words, an opening prayer, a request for donations, or merely asking for a vote. I have no doubt that my voice quavered every time I stood up in middle school student council and read my treasurer's report. In my mind, it was a whispery voice with a full quaver, but as no one ever asked me to repeat myself (and middle schoolers are not famous for their merciful attitude towards their peers) it can't have been that quiet. How ever tough it is for you, your audience is full of people who are thrilled you're up there speaking—not them. As a result, they will always be kind in their assessment.

As you get braver and want to speak your own thoughts, ask yourself hard questions. Are you the right person to present? Does your audience need anything in advance? Do they need background on the issue or you or can you just cut to the chase? PowerPoint may need to be part of your academic and professional life, but try to present without using it as often as you can. The most compelling presenters are the ones who can tell you the story and keep you interested. I'm a huge fan of Sheryl Sandberg's TED Talk, "Why We Have Too Few Women Leaders" that has no graphics. She believes enough in her message to trust it. Note that the best speakers in the world with amazing new ideas get 20 minutes or less to give their TED talk. There's probably no scenario where you need to be anywhere near as long as that. Keep in mind that some ideas are best presented by someone else or with someone else. Can't think of who could deliver the message with as much care and attention to details as you? Then you're the right person. Think about the audience and the power structures in play and consider the best way to accomplish your goals. Don't have a goal? Even as simple as expressing your opinion on the short story the class read? It's okay to start small and present one-on-one just by saying after class, "Hey, I loved that you defended that idea." Do that every so often and you will help to create a supportive culture, which is exactly what you'll want when you get brave enough to present to the group.

Some of my favorite groups on campuses that offer a ton of organizing, meetings, and on stage speaking opportunities are campus TEDx events, coffee house open mic nights, anything with officers—student council, the Greek system, intramural sports, political groups, and interfaith efforts. Keep in mind that with Greek systems and your own faith, you will deal exclusively with a self-selected group with very common values and priorities. These are great places to start out and build a foundation of success, but be sure to branch out. Religious groups on campus will always have some involvement with an interfaith council, which will perpetually ask you to consider different viewpoints. Events like an interfaith week give you a chance to not only organize and speak to something you feel passionately about, but they also provide a great chance to provide support for other, different viewpoints. In the work world, the best ideas and execution of those ideas are going to come out in a diverse group. You want the troubleshooting to happen internally, not months or years later by customers as an expensive idea fails in the marketplace.

Speak One-on-one

One of the things I've really noticed as I've gotten to know students at the University of Puget Sound is just how many adults they have in their lives and how, over the four college years, they get better at speaking with me as a peer. They are assigned an advisor during orientation who gets to know them and helps them pick their classes. They keep that advisor and acquire at least one more in their major. They can trade advisors if they find a better match or just add another one. Many students have multiple majors, minors, or concentrations: more advisors. There's a fellowship office and a career services office. There are advisors for extracurriculars as well as coaches for the athletic teams. There's an interfaith advisor. These are all places they acquire adult friends just as naturally as they make peer friends. Once you go into the workplace, you've got to be able to hold your own in a conversation with your boss, clients, and vendors. Everyone is probably older and more experienced than you, so if you're still thinking (and speaking) like a high school senior to a teacher, you're slowing yourself way down.

Some students get this experience as a result of being naturally outgoing. Other students have jobs on campus that require practicing these skills. If you have a hard time talking to adults, practicing this skill can feel insurmountable. At any school you should be able to start by talking to professors. Make an effort to go to office hours at least once for every class for some reason other than your grade in the class. If your professors are adjunct faculty or grad students, they are still adults, and the principle will hold. Ask the professor how they got interested in the subject, what they think the best elective in their field is on campus, what other professors are not to be missed, what's the most common mistake they see undergraduates make with their time on campus. Your goal is to have a conversation with them as another human being. You can even confess to college staff that you're trying to get better at speaking to adults as peers.

Talk to your resident advisor (RA), usually an upperclassman on your floor. Find out what they like about the job, what the biggest mistakes they see freshmen make are, and what their major is. I'm sorry to say that I made no such effort my freshman year in the dorms and can tell you nothing about the RAs on my floor. If nothing else, becoming a real person to them and seeing them as real people is likely to make for a smoother year in your home away from home.

Seek out the tutoring center on campus. College writing is very different from high school writing, and even excellent students find they need to make adjustments to be academically successful at a college level. Many average students find, despite being accepted to college, that they may have to take a remedial writing class to get them up to speed. (If this is true for you, and your school does not give credit for these classes, see if there is anything you can do the summer before college. It's very expensive to be taking non-credit classes during the semesters you are paying tuition.) Most schools are very proud of their freshman writing seminars. These are all natural times to seek out a writing tutor, typically a peer, working in the writing center. Working together over a shared project is very close to the way you will work after college. Any chance to get feedback, ask questions, and improve your work not only helps academically right now, but gives you a chance to practice the kind of one-on-one speaking that's required to prepare any proposal or presentation. Even if you are an excellent writer, writing for a class outside your field can require a different approach. As college progresses you may become an excellent science, philosophy, business, or English writer, but when you take an elective class in another subject, a writing tutor with expertise can help you adjust your work for another kind of audience. If you have the chance to work as a tutor, whether paid or as a volunteer, it's a job well worth having because you will meet a wide variety of students. Each will have different skills, personalities, and goals, and working with all those people will inevitably help you develop skills in dealing with all those variables, as well as give you a unique chance to provide negative feedback in a positive manner. This will be an invaluable skill in the workplace and throughout your career—one for which there is very little opportunity to train.

ORGANIZE

ORGANIZE PEOPLE

As you're going through academic life, it's common to think organizing people is easy. Class meetings are mandatory, lab hours are set and finite. Those who fail to show up for class, Monday chapter meetings, competitions, or auditions, are naturally failed out of school, get called to standards, cut from the team, or don't get to perform. In the real world, it's a lot harder to guarantee everyone has the same openings in their schedules. At work, people have different schedules or are in different time zones. In volunteering they have different gaps in their personal and work obligations. This is one reason why I strongly encourage fraternity and sorority members to prioritize working in other campus groups as well. Sororities and fraternities have strong national organizational rules to enforce their culture and you really need to develop the skills to make things happen. There will be times when you have no power and there may be no enforceable consequences to people ducking your meetings. Any campus group will require that there be meetings and that you set goals for the meetings, the semester, the year, or over a multiyear schedule. To meet those goals, you'll need to divide your resources, set up committees, break the work into chunks, and delegate some to other people. Classwork will require that you organize, but much of the time it will just be you prioritizing your own resources, and I'm advocating that you get used to organizing other people as well.

In addition to organizing, by setting goals over different time-lines and also ceding absolute control over the success or failure of a venture, you'll start facing the need to follow up with other people, compromise on timing and even quality, avert disasters, re-delegate, and lobby for support from the larger group. You'll learn to compromise to accomplish larger goals. You'll find out what works and what doesn't in managing people, tasks, and even in up-front goal setting. You may be sure the clear priority for the group is the capstone annual event, while others are sure that it's developing a September kickoff event for the following year. You may be willing to win support for the capstone event with a compromise of devoting your summer to working on the kick off as well, and still not be able to sway the group. And then your role as a leader may be to switch gears and admit that this year the capstone event will be a toned-down affair or even canceled, to enable the group to shift to the kickoff. Learning to be open to a different point of view, or even execute a world-class plan for a final outcome you don't personally advocate, is a great experience. The beauty of these experiments in college is that failure is not fatal. If the kick off doesn't attract enough participants, in part because you didn't have the capstone event to bring the group together before the summer break, then you just convene the group and redirect for the next year. Having an experience like that to discuss in an interview gives an interviewer really great, positive insights into how you handle the real world where plans change. Talking through what worked or didn't work and improving going forward is valuable experience for everyone.

Organizing Members

Formal membership processes in a group provide built-in consequences for members complying with the formal leadership's vision and action plan. In these groups, you can learn a lot about working with a small leadership team and be confident that once the board speaks, the membership will comply. When your groups have structured to include officers, it can be great to hold those titles, but only if there is real value in the work. What constitutes real value? If you are secretary, be sure you know how to take good notes. Meeting notes are valuable only if they provide exactly enough information. They need enough information to have historical, record-keeping value, but not a transcript of every discussion. Do your notes conclude with action items, including those responsible and their deadlines? If your group simply hands the secretary the position with no guidance or asks that you serve as a court reporter to capture the entire transcription, it's not a job that translates to a valuable skill in the professional world. A secretary's notes should be very concise, provide an outline of the subjects discussed and any conclusions, whether those are motions or action items (but not the entire discussion leading up to those motions or action items). You can easily be the secretary who helps your organization make the shift to keeping valuable minutes, but be sure that goal is shared by the rest of the board. They may like their long-winded minutes, but there's just no reason for you to take on that job. If you are vice president, be sure you have real responsibilities for the task at hand. If your position doesn't have a timeline, develop one for the next person. What has to happen each month? If you are vice president for a subset, like communications or fundraising, be sure you know what goals the position has and that you are interested in fulfilling those successfully. Being vice president of philanthropy when your job is to make two rote donations voted on by the membership isn't very impressive, despite the title. Assume for any title you put on your résumé that an interviewer will treat that like an actual job. They will ask what you did. They will look for metrics, so if you would be forced to confess it was an easy gig with no real responsibility for money, people, or goals, then it's a potential negative. Rather than impress, it's going to backfire and make you look like you don't know how to work effectively or accurately assess a situation. Neither of these traits is desirable in a potential employee. A president should be running the group, carving out strategic goals, enlisting support, ensuring the organization is meeting its goals now ,and setting up for success in future years. If your president gig is awarded to a senior who then calls the group to order at monthly meetings, that's not nearly as impressive as a more generic title. If the coordinator of the student comedy night has a real budget for a real event and has to fill a specific number of slots, and deal with last-minute weather and health issues, the coordinator position is the more impressive. Be sure the title reflects the work. If you can't have a conversation about the position and explain all the things you managed and learned, even some disasters, whether averted or not, then the title shouldn't even be on your résumé as you look for internships and jobs.

One of the draws for my son, Nick, with the University of Puget Sound was hearing about their student-run orientation. A nine-day experience, it truly is student-run and the process for becoming a leader in subsequent years is quite competitive. For me, as a parent looking at colleges, the draw of the award-winning, student-run anything is what those adjectives say about the culture. This is a school whose brand is all about letting the students set the tone, and this is reflected throughout the choices and opportunities they provide. The students who lead those groups have very real responsibilities. They work very hard for two weeks to make the orientation a successful launch for all the incoming students, acclimating them to a new place, new activities, new friends, and in exchange they get housing, food, and a very small, token stipend. What they think they get is an incredible bonding experience as they hustle to make the whole thing come together to be amazing every year. No matter who the audience, and regardless of whatever obstacles the weather and the rest of the universe throws at them, they bond as leaders by going through it together. What I know they get is rock-solid experience running meetings, planning events with budgets, welcoming new, different people into their community, and terrific fodder for winning interview conversations.

Organizing Volunteers

Organizing true volunteers, people not bound by any membership requirements or paycheck, is another, different opportunity to seek out. By the time you are an experienced leader on campus, you will inevitably see gaps or problems that you want to address. Even something as simple as a scheduled Saturday morning beach trash pickup can derail when half your volunteers don't show up because of traffic or a summer rainstorm. Handling that frustration, resetting goals, and making the day a positive experience for those who did show, should give you a sense of accomplishment, even if you covered less ground or picked up less pounds of trash than you had previously planned. Delegating tasks, creating more leaders on the fly, and maximizing the group's chance of success are all achievements for a leader. When things don't go exactly as planned, do take the time to consider what lessons you learned, and what things you did accomplish. Research shows that taking a positive look, finding things to appreciate, and cultivating gratitude will make you a happier person. As a rule, if you consider taking on anything, given the shortage of time many college student have, consider what two to three points you could make if you were discussing this activity afterwards. Write those down! If you decide it's worthwhile then move forward. If you need help with evaluating experiences, I have a planning sheet you can download at LaunchLikeARocket.com/plan.

Once your group has a stable foundation, whether you inherited or created it, you should try and grow it. Growth is a core goal in most organizations, so this is a great chance to practice. In an off-shoot group without a formal hiring or recruitment process to ensure your numbers each year, this will let you experiment with ways that might help to spread the word. If your events have been too group focused, you may find your profile on campus is too low to continue to attract new members to sustain, much less grow, the group. If you go into your activities knowing you need to gain experience in sales and growth, you'll think about these issues and plan with an eye to this eventual need. You may even be able to see this need within your academic department. While colleges have an abundance of students who are interested in psychology and economics, they sometimes have a harder time filling their philosophy, classics, and religious studies classes. If you are in a major you love that has this kind of problem, it might be a great opportunity to create a group, working closely with your professors, to generate some interest. Colleges don't necessarily need more students to change their major to one of these, but they do need students to fill the classes each semester, so engaging just a small portion of your peers to experiment and try an introductory survey class can have a big impact on the health of your department. If your professors show no interest in an initiative like this, I'd recommend you stick with the major but double down on finding adult mentors in other areas. You need to learn from people focused on the long-term sustainability of their organization, and not everyone has that skill set.

Occasionally you'll find a group that relies upon a small set of people, or even one person, for its success. The group will be quite content with this state of affairs. In the work world that's a recipe for a major failure. The organization would be far too vulnerable to a lightning bolt from the blue—a new job offer, a health issue, a geographic relocation, or just the whim of their charismatic leader. Potential future leaders would quickly assess the situation and move on, so there'd be little talent in the pipeline, further increasing the dependence on the current leadership. Student-led college organizations, particularly newer clubs without the larger support infrastructure of the Greek system or intramural athletics, can be vulnerable to this kind of disruption. As you move into senior year, if you've been a good manager of people as a sophomore and junior, you should have several clear choices for successors. Ideally they can begin to take the reins from you now. At least by second semester they should run the show with you acting in a purely advisory position. If nothing else, your senior year has the whole bonus time-consuming task of applying to graduate school or career positions, so you will need your time freed up to tackle those tasks anyway. If you want to leave any kind of legacy or just protect your reputation, it's important to leave behind a sustainable organization. Even in an organization with a strong structure that recognizes the four-year cycle of college leaders, you need to be sure you're empowering your organizationally structured successors to be successful.

The number-one problem we see with new college grads, even athletes used to working on a team, is a failure to plan for someone else to step into your workload on a moment's notice. I see this in a failure to leave notes with key information in Slack, relevant emails or communications not copied to our shared server where they belong for group reference, and updated information unrecorded in our job tracking sheet. While simple word processing application files might be fine as-is, we see our more complicated technical Adobe application files that work to export finished files, but when opened, don't clearly show where someone left off. I'm confident that when a project is finished, most conscientious people tidy up and leave a neat package behind. In a work environment the switch may occur well before the end, before you've had a chance to tidy up, so your process has to leave that same tidy trail at all stages. Even if you're never sick, late, pulled into a meeting, or on vacation, someday you'll leave the company. That's when someone else opens up your file to make a quick update and discovers the file isn't well-built. Your reputation takes a beating, although you will never know it. Be sure you're not this person in your management of tasks. All the tasks on your plate are also chances to manage people above and below you, even if you can't see that from your starting point. Be certain you're thinking big picture and long term. As hard as it is to imagine, you won't really feel all that excited about fielding emails and texts about the homecoming planning process three months after graduation when you are trying to get acclimated to your new life. Groom a successor early on and they'll flush out all the little glitches in your notes and files before you've left campus.

ORGANIZE TIME AND SCHEDULES

Your Time

Inevitably everyone learns to manage their time in college, but that doesn't mean you learn how to do it well. If you're coming into junior year still writing papers at the last minute or staying up all night to study for midterms, regardless of the academic success you may be achieving, you're not managing your time well. In the working world, your boss wants to see the finished product, weigh in for revisions, and make major adjustments based on late-breaking information. There's a big difference in perception if your supervisor goes home with your work product on their desk for a morning meeting compared to knowing you'll deliver in plenty of time late tonight. They may know it, but that doesn't mean that they don't worry. And if your boss is spending any time at all worrying about your work getting done, you're not managing perceptions very well, even if you think you're managing your time satisfactorily. This is fundamentally different than the educational process. In education, as long as you turn it on time, you get the grade your work deserves. Sure, we can argue that the work might be better quality if you had more time for revisions or proofreading, but your professors only care about their deadline. Even at the small colleges with the highest faculty-to-student ratios, the most involved professors are used to students turning in work one minute before the deadline as well as five days late. They might like you and feel bad you missed the deadline or cut it close, but they didn't worry about all their students right up until the deadline hit. Their feelings reflect the fact that individual students' actions don't impact their careers in a big way. The personal stake in your output is just not the same as when your boss is counting on you. In the workplace pyramid, your teammates and supervisors are building on your work, so they are selfishly much more concerned about your progress. That's why a dependable last-minute miracle delivery of quality work just isn't going to get the same kind of reward as the same work delivered (via reliable progress reports) a little early.

If you look closely at the experience of working on teams arranging extracurricular activities, you'll find the same group dynamics at work. The people who are thought to be highly reliable will be handling their tasks in a transparent manner. Progress will be regular and visible. Bottlenecks and concerns will be tackled by the group in meetings. As much as a last-minute save might be appreciated in the moment, that last-minute delivery of the finished fliers for an event isn't going to give you the same kind of reputation for reliability. They may know you always come through, but they won't feel safe delegating to you—that worried feeling will rule their overall perception of you, so be sure to factor it into your behavior.

By joining groups in college and moving beyond participant roles, whether producing events or leading at the board level, you'll be able to watch the dynamics. See who wins respect and has a strong reputation and pay attention to what they are doing differently than other people. Building this cultural perception skill will serve you in good stead in any work environment. Asking how you can help, taking direction, delivering on your promises, and then training the next person in that role, will all help you build your time management skills.

In setting your goals within a group, always under-promise and over-deliver. If you think you can get the program or budget done by Wednesday next week, suggest Friday as a deadline. Things happen in life—you'll wake up with the flu one day, have a new project assigned in a class, or find a speaker is on campus that you really can't pass up. If you allow for those disruptions, you'll comfortably hit the promised deadline. If the work is easy to do, you get a lucky break. If no competing priority arises, you'll beat the deadline. Even if you can't move the meeting earlier, you now have time to email it over so the rest of the team can review in advance or seek out feedback from one particularly trusted source, so the work is even better by Friday.

While you're in college, you're going to pick a major, maybe change it, add new interests, and the college is going to be adding and subtracting majors, courses, and other opportunities. Or maybe the college itself just isn't the fit you thought it would be and you need to look at transferring. That's just the academic side of long-term planning. Be sure to factor in changes in your activities: sports, clubs, Greek life, and perhaps a semester (or more) abroad. By junior year you should be looking at relevant certifications your school might offer and making time to investigate whatever no-credit career services workshops or appointments they have. Your jobs may have to be less about solely generating income and more focused on trying out future careers, building skills, and developing a network. It's tempting to continue as a nanny for the flexible hours or extra hours on weekend nights, as a waiter earning tips, or in a store for the employee discount. It can be much easier to keep working on campus in the interest of daily time management—that's probably the shortest commute you'll ever have. But you may need to cut back a bit on those jobs to make time for an unpaid internship in a field that interests you, or spend a summer in a lower-paid, but more career-relevant job. And planning for that junior summer income hit means you may need to spend the school year working an extra shift to cover the drop in income that summer. Or maybe you take the internship for the weekdays and get a weekend job. Yes, it's tough to spend 10–12 summer weeks with no days off. But it's even tougher to graduate and have an infinite number of days off because you haven't gained employable skills.

Over time, you're going to find that some groups you loved just aren't a great fit any longer. Maybe they've changed, maybe you've changed. We all know we have to clean out our closet sometime—get rid of the clothes that don't fit, are hopelessly out of style, don't suit our activities, or that we just don't like to wear. But somehow it's much harder to admit we've outgrown people and activities. That's probably a good thing overall if we're worrying that other people might feel judged or have their feelings hurt. But it's a really bad thing if you're letting old activities consume your limited time and distort your changing priorities. Dropping a group doesn't mean you have to drop the people, although you should be aware it may play out that way. A common complaint about the

Greek system on college campuses is that it is so activity-rich that it consumes all its members' time. And that means they don't have time left for outsiders. The same can be true of college athletic teams. The tendency of people in these all-consuming groups to room together further closes the social circle. So when you decide you need to exit a group like that, you're right to imagine it's going to cost you friends. And some people may be mad, because if you're saying this activity isn't a smart use of your time and they suspect the same thing might be true for them, you're putting them in a really uncomfortable spot inside their own heads. This experience can be as much about managing people as it is time.

In a work environment, if you stay too long in any complacent, low-achieving environment, you're going to move toward the mean and become that kind of worker. It's a pretty standard trope in self-improvement circles that you are the average of the five people you spend the most time with (and coworkers have a leg up on logging the time with you to make that short list). In college you're going to have to juggle and it's a great chance to get the skills you'll need to leave with grace. Once you go to work, you may find your dream job eventually becomes a bad fit for helping you achieve your next set of goals. Your current college community might be great but the biology department is a tough environment due to all the pre-med students viewing each other as competition. Stay a biology major, of course, but join some friendlier groups on campus. Outdoor programs are a pretty reliably laid-back, accepting crowd but sometimes unconsciously demand a high level of fitness. It's hard to find any interfaith group that won't provide a set of very welcoming people focused on improving themselves while focused on accepting the differences between people and interested in new viewpoints, but they tend not to have a representative group of atheists. Look around carefully and you'll find something to balance out any anticipated deficits in your social life as a result of moving on from an activity.

There's an art to leaving environments that aren't working for you any longer. This isn't the moment for you to let forth with your honest opinion. If you're leaving mock trial, no matter why, just say you've got some other interests you want to pursue, you've learned what you wanted to from this experience, or there are some other things you want to check out before you graduate. There's nothing gained by airing a list of grievances publicly or privately. You've decided to leave, it's too late for them to change things and woo you back, so let it all go. When you leave a job, it's much the same drill. You should be saying that you're leaving for a geographic move, a new opportunity, for a new job that will build on your skills (that you are "so happy to have had a chance to learn"). Basically, it's a version of breaking up saying, "It's not you, it's me." You just want to get out as cleanly and neatly as possible so you can get back to spending your time on current priorities.

By the way, it's perfectly appropriate to go see campus mental health services to talk through the emotional side of leaving. You don't have to be on the edge of a breakdown to benefit from a little counseling. They would love to help you figure out how to tell your freshman year roommate you don't want to stay together as sophomores. It's not all serious problems in counseling—lots of people are just doing a reality check or getting an objective view of a sticky issue. And if you are distraught because you were recruited and drawn to the school entirely because you thought you'd play lacrosse or sing and those are the only people you know—every other group you are in is a spoke off that hub and leaving the group may cost you all your friends—definitely go see them. This is why they are there. I promise you that they will reiterate that you have not ruined your life, you are not alone, you do not need to transfer, nor are you trapped forever by some wrong turns made earlier.

And if you are realizing you have made a significant wrong turn, don't be shy about involving other adults in your life. You may need to reach out to your high school coach, the admissions office at another school that accepted you, or even your parents to get a clear perspective, advice, or just some support. A former coach can give you great advice on how to talk to a current coach. Many schools will honor an acceptance from a year ago and some will even honor any merit aid award as well. There are a certain number of students who don't show up freshman year, and a few, like you, who decide their chosen school is too far away from home, too expensive, too cold, too humid, too much of a party school, or too academic at the expense of campus social life. Colleges would love nothing better than to have you step into one of those empty spots, created by someone with feelings much like yours, who also had the courage to admit that things weren't going as well as they could. You just have to let people know what's going on to find out what all your options are.

Their Time

Assuming you are the complete master of your schedule of commitments, now you need to layer in managing your life in concert with everyone else's. You need to move from being the perfectly tuned cellist in the orchestra to being the conductor. That takes time and practice. Your college social life will let you continue to coordinate with your friends but it does add complexity. As compared to high school, everyone has different class hours, and some of those may be evening labs, while more people will have jobs that eat up evenings and weeknights. For example, admissions offices usually have a set of overnight hosts for prospective students, so now you have friends who effectively have jobs that entail working from 8:00 p.m.–8:00 a.m. with relatively short notice. Other friends might be resident assistants, who also have 24-hour shifts of on-call hours and unexpected emergencies. Throw in some of the traditional initiation rites for clubs, and you now have a last-minute cancellation or no-show situation that didn't come into play in high school. (Although it is pretty similar to work, when your coworkers can have family responsibilities for sick children, delayed flights, or car trouble on the way into the office.) Your family life is more complicated. If your family home is two hours from the airport, you definitely now need to coordinate holiday travel to and from home with your siblings or other out-of-town family members. It was definitely easier when you woke up in the right place on Thanksgiving day or flew to spend the weekend with your dad on a ticket he'd arranged.

If your parents are still helicoptering in and arranging all of this stuff, it's a major missed opportunity and you will need to fight them off. As busy as school seems and as much as your mom or dad loves to take care of you, you'll be busier at work and your manager won't ever dream of checking you into your flight 24 hours in advance or paying for early check-in, but will be frustrated, if not angry, when you are the one person who gets bumped off an oversold flight. If you miss a connection or your flight gets canceled you need to figure out how to fix it. Setting things up and fixing small problems now, when you have more time, and maybe access to your parent's credit card, is all skill-building. When things go wrong at work, you can't always duck into the bathroom and call for advice. You've got to think on your feet. Every time you practice thinking about how the pieces come together for family events in a scenario where you are not the center of the universe, you gain real skills. Don't miss these chances. Stop considering the holidays as events put on for you by your adoring fans and consider yourself a staffer whose job requires attendance with a minimum of fuss and no intervention by the boss. Not only will you build skills, but the sooner you appear to your parents as an adult family member, the earlier they will give you the respect they give to the competent adults whose company they enjoy at family events. Maybe you can even stop sitting at the kids' table!

Professors and other college staff are generally viewed by students as managers, perhaps as peers when you are working alongside them in a lab or as a teaching assistant (TA). If you view professors, college administrators, and career services staff as managers, you'll find lots of opportunities to juggle your schedule to make it convenient for them to meet with you. For the most part, they will be on a more traditional 8:00 a.m.–5:00 p.m. working schedule. Certainly even those teaching an evening class are less likely to want to meet after the class at 9:00 p.m., however convenient that solution might seem to be in terms of your schedules and geography. They are not undergraduate students and keep a more standard post-college work schedule. Even graduate students are likely to prefer getting back to their own labs, coursework, research, or writing to having coffee after class to discuss your academic progress or career plans.

Overcoming any intimidation you feel about requesting some of their undivided attention is the first skill. College is a chance to be both a teenager and an adult nearly simultaneously. Despite much evidence that you are still a teenager, in your interactions with adults you should be operating immediately and seamlessly as another adult. In many cases you'll be on a first-name basis, although the rules of politeness in most cases will require that you wait for Professor Johnson to tell you to call her Jane. With graduate student TAs who are several years older, feel free to ask if it's not clear. They are likely still making the shift themselves to the next stage of adulthood and may not have worked out their preferences or defaults. There is no one right answer and figuring out how to navigate that world, how to claim as much equality as you are entitled to, but not so much you alienate a higher-up, is one of the things that continues to vary across cultures—national, regional, industry, and company.

Once you've figured out how to address a manager, you want to get some practice reaching out and getting meetings for feedback, projects, or advice. Once again, you want to get practice, but not be annoying, so don't do more than you need. Many students never show up during office hours, or if they do, they show up to debate a half-point credit on a paper or test. Show up to ask questions about the field or the professor's work. Much like a good date, you don't want to spend the whole time talking about yourself. Find out what the other person is interested in. Ask questions. Then go off on your own and evaluate if that's a fit for you. It may well be that a particularly promising professor has no interest in undergraduates or in mentoring, or is about to leave for a sabbatical just as you are going into upper division classes. You are going to have some misses—professors who don't have the time, interest, or skills to be mentors or staffers who just have no knowledge about working in your field or in the Pacific Northwest, for example, despite being expert in career development.

Scheduling initial meetings with people who might be helpful and finding out how they might help doesn't involve you talking about yourself. It involves you finding out about them. You are the one who needs to start putting the pieces together to make a map for your life. The way to do that is to find potential guides and mentors, arrange meetings, and figure it out. For example, if there's no one in the film department who can tie your Cinema Studies major into a career and no one in the career office to advise you, then you should be working on getting together a group of similarly situated students and asking the administration for guidance on how to fix the situation. Is there an alumni or parent who might be invited to speak at school, join a conference call, or participate in a Q&A in some fashion? Finding these gaps on campus is a project to start early in your college career, so your work to address the deficiency can directly benefit your career. With a world that changes quickly and a constantly shifting set of students and student preferences, every college will have gaps in their opportunities, as will every place you work. Managing your time, not only over a semester, but in the context of your four years, and in relation to the college's staffers and the department's planning processes, is a great introduction into the real world. Having just missed the budget planning process for the year because you were busy or just had your great idea is a normal part of life. It will happen again, no matter how expert you become at maneuvering any system. The key is to know how to get back on track when you need to coordinate not only with higher-ups but within the workings of a bureaucracy.

Our Time

Your college career is a finite thing. Ideally you have a four-year time frame, while the school itself has a plan for the year and a multiyear strategic plan. Everything planned and unplanned competes for time, attention, and money. It's your community, but it's one you will leave in a relatively short period of time. One of the things you should be looking at is how you manage not only your time in college, organizing it all with other people's to meet this week's and next month's needs, but what your contribution to the community will be over the course of your time there. As an adult, it's reasonable to expect that you will make a contribution to the community. If you were lucky enough to grow up in a neighborhood where parents coached Little League, chaperoned field trips, donated to the church bake sale, or worked for school fundraisers, you've had some strong role models. Be cognizant that investing in a community is what makes it great for both the current and future generations.

As you manage your time, keep an eye out for ways to improve the community for the long haul. If there's a gap in the information from career services and the biology department on the career path to veterinary medicine school, try and fix it for good. It's great for you and your cohorts to get a local veterinarian to come talk or a representative from a veterinary school to visit, but leave a road map for fixing the problem permanently. However small the fix, even if it's clearly an incomplete solution, try not to make it a one-time thing. If you called seven veterinarians and five schools to acquire that one speaker, be sure to leave those planning notes for another student to take over, particularly if you can't get your academic institution to take on the responsibility. See if you can get a group of aspiring veterinary students to form a club and meet once a semester to keep your group's needs in the eye of the departments and administrators.

If you start a club or an event or take over something existing, take the long view. While you may be able to pull it off single-handedly, not everyone will have your unique combination of skills and free time. If there's a gap between your graduation and the next person, the community will be the weaker. Someone else who is willing to start over from scratch is a much tougher find than a student who builds on your hard work. Your view of organizing and planning should include a few thoughts for how the event can continue in your absence. If you inherited it and it was absolutely perfect with templates for everything on a flash drive, move it to Google Drive or Dropbox. Introduce Slack or Evernote. Even the most perfect event will be impacted by new and improved technological solutions. Both you and your skills will be enhanced. Even a failed implementation helps the group understand what kinds of innovations might be worthwhile and which didn't work. These kinds of long-term, strategic initiatives are exactly what businesses and other organizations need to try to evolve and succeed. Gaining experience developing plans that cross over from one semester to another and with a volunteer turnover that will presumably be about 25 percent is a unique opportunity to build almost every soft skill a business could ever need, as well as some practical hard skills in applications and workflow tools.

ORGANIZE MONEY

Develop Budgets

While it may initially feel you simply have no money and nothing to manage, money management is one of the most fundamental skills to acquire. No matter what you do professionally in later life, however much or little money you make, if you can manage it well, you'll be happier at home and more successful at work.

Many four-year schools require freshmen to live in campus housing with a meal plan, and perhaps you'll have a limited amount of spending money handed out from your parents. Even in that context, with incredibly controlling parents, you can begin to take control of your finances. While you may not feel your allowance or earnings are such that they require an actual written budget, a budget is a commitment to yourself, and if only for that reason, it is worth writing down a basic plan. After consulting with many parents with students in college, we arrived at a $200 monthly allowance number. Nick's freshman year this money was automatically transferred into his account and he made it work out for his social life. Even with no real need-based expenses and lots of activities on campus, $50 a week won't let you see many movies or eat out all that often. If you're running out at the end of the month, that's pretty normal, but figure out how to make it work. Jake had the same number and spent most of freshman year supplementing from his savings (too many meals outside of the cafeteria as a result of wanting dinner late at night when the dorm cafeteria wasn't an option). Looking at his expenditures didn't require any apps or spreadsheets to see where he needed to cut back. A job that netted him $50–75 a month would put him back in balance if he didn't want to cut back. There are, after all, only two ways to balance a budget: cut your spending or increase your income.

If you're working while going to college or living at home doing the first two years of general education at a community college, you're naturally going to have a lot more opportunity to master your budgeting. Prioritize your spending if you're not firmly backed by an affluent set of parents or grandparents. Understanding the difference between a need and a want is a major step towards a financially savvy life. If it's not a true need (shelter, food, weather-required clothing, tuition, books, transportation), then it's a want. Consider whether doing or having it will be meaningful two or four years out. As much as a given social event seems all-important in the moment, most prove not to be vital in the long run. The summer after my graduation from business school, still looking for a job in the entertainment industry during the longest-running writers' strike, one of my very close friends was getting married on the East Coast. All my friends were going and they even offered to put me on a pull-out bed in one of their hotel rooms, but still living off my parents, with student loans about to start requiring payments, I just couldn't risk putting my flight on a credit card, so I didn't go. My friends understood, and when everyone reminisces about that weekend, we laugh about how poor we all were—and that I was so poor I couldn't come. Life is long, and even for your closest friends, sometimes you won't be able to get to every truly important event. Your own child will be sick, your brother will be getting married the same weekend, you'll be presenting at a conference, or just not be able to afford it. Have fun, don't say no to everything, but don't say yes to everything if those memories require extensive use of a credit card you'll be paying off a decade later.

Nick did so well managing his money freshman year that in subsequent years we arrived at a figure for the whole school year that covered allowance, flights home for the holidays, and books. We transferred all the money in one lump sum each August. If you can manage that weekly or monthly amount well enough, suggest this approach to your parents. Deciding what you can afford, weighing the convenience versus cost of certain flights, used versus new text-books, and hustling for a ride to the airport instead of a shuttle, Uber, or a cab are all real-world decisions you'll be making with your own money for the rest of your life.

If you need a job, consider working in the financial aid office for your school. Just hearing the questions prospective students and their parents ask and seeing the number of your fellow students dealing with their aid will be incredibly instructive. It's never too soon to see that money can cause a lot of stress. To the extent you can understand how borrowing and lending works, common pitfalls, and how people manage their money, the better off your are for creating your own framework.

In addition to managing your own money, seek out opportunities to manage a group budget. Even at small liberal arts colleges the total associated students groups typically control a six-figure budget. At UCLA, with one of the largest student groups in the United States, ASUCLA controls a multimillion dollar annual budget. They manage the student union building on campus as well as the undergraduate and graduate student governments. According to *The Daily Bruin*, their 2015-2016 budget included an allocation of $3,000,000 for improvements to the student union building, Ackerman Union. No matter the size of your school or student government, participating in the process of allocating significant funds is a great experience. Even if your interests don't run to a treasurer position, leadership in almost any group will need to petition or propose their requirements for the club's part of the overall budget. Once the budget is ascertained, just like Jake's personal budget quandary freshman year, you either have to cut back on planned expenditures or find a way to increase revenues.

Within any group, the process of collectively managing money and making group decisions might prove to be more valuable than actually managing the money. The group is full of individuals, each of whom has different preferences, personal financial wherewithal, available time, and levels of commitment. Balancing all those things and finding a way to manage the money effectively will require people management as much as budget management. That's the big value-add. If your group is largely affluent or school supported (as with an athletic team), there's not much value. Remember, I'm not proposing these ideas as tasks you check off your to-do list to build a résumé. You've already proven you can do that with your high school efforts earning you a college acceptance. I'm saying you need to encounter messy problems and find imperfect solutions, or simply be unable to find solutions down one path and have to redirect. Put yourself in tough situations, where the answer isn't obvious or may be need to be fluid, or even where a significant compromise is required because all the constituencies can't agree. This is what will happen in life and your career over and over again. There's no situation when an organization with serious goals, whether simply profit or curing cancer or preventing malaria, is going to chase all possible options with the same level of commitment. Businesses make bets on the future in the narrow band of priorities they pursue, schools decide which departments they will nurture, scientists decide where the most promise might be to solve big problems. Money and time are finite, and somehow a group has to agree what avenues they are pursuing.

If you can, find an opportunity to get involved with the university's own goals, whether through admissions, development (fundraising), or senior campus administration, such as a president, chancellor, or dean's office, the numbers will get bigger and you'll see the truth is that there's never enough money on the table to meet all possible requests. At the institutional level you'll get to see multiyear strategic plans in use. Colleges are always somewhere in the creation or revision stage, while a previous plan is still being implemented. The process requires many levels of buy in from below and above. Even your college's president or chancellor has a board of trustees they report to, who in turn may be beholden to donors or state taxpayers and has to win the support of department chairs to implement change. Even a low-level, part-time student job in any level of the university would let you see the real-world prioritization of all those needs and wants, building a buffer for unexpected problems or opportunities, building out a multiyear plan, and implementing it in an ever-changing world. Not only are the school's donations or enrollments going down or up unexpectedly, but the demands of students, parents, employers, alumni, and donors are also changing based on their best bet for what they think our collective future holds, while the endowment investments generating a portion of the school's revenue are also returning a fluctuating amount. All this requires a massive amount of managing expectations as much as actual money. While I doubt there are many student jobs, paid or volunteer, that let you be involved in the decisions, simply helping to host events for any of these constituencies and overhearing those conversations would yield big-picture insights you won't otherwise be able to access until you're a decade into your career. Access to these kind of conversations is one reason why a job with the college's newspaper, magazine, or radio station could prove to be incredibly valuable. With a little journalism credibility, you've got the ability to reach out to anyone involved with the college and start asking questions. You want the kind of insights you can't get on your own, through direct experience, so you can be aware those exist as you make your own career choices.

Make Sales

Students who work their way through college, or at least work a part-time job, have some advantage here in getting the most fundamental skill of all: the ability to sell. Everyone has to sell in their career. You'll have to sell ideas within your organization, or sell yourself to an organization or manager, even if you never actually have to sell to your organization's audience. Find opportunities to practice selling directly to an audience. Whether it's selling tickets for a group on campus, a summer spent in a restaurant or retail environment, or working for admissions on campus, having some idea of how a direct, transactional, immediate sale works will be invaluable. Selling requires reading your audience, pushing without being pushy, naming a price for the thing you are selling, and perhaps collecting on that promise to buy (or pay).

Every college in the U.S. has a development (fundraising) office, and usually once or twice a year they have students make phone calls to raise money from parents and alumni. They'll have a great training program with scripts and all the prospects lined up for you. You'll be surrounded by other students tackling the same job. If sales isn't your thing or this is incredibly hard for you, the camaraderie will make it bearable.

If the theatre department doesn't sell all the tickets to a performance, they are still going to have the performance. If no one comes to the swim meet, the meet will still go on. There is literally no downside to failing in your sales efforts for these kinds of events, so if you can't find anything else that interests you, pick an event like this and try to find ways to increase ticket sales and attendance. Selling is something you have to experience to learn and it's much better to gain these basic skills when the support infrastructure is so strong.

Generate Profit

While I'll leave the idea of basic business and money management to other books and blogs, I do want to touch on the basic language of business. Any organization will have a balance sheet, a quick snapshot of a moment in time that lists its assets, equity, and liabilities. In accounting the basic equation when people talk about their books balancing is the idea that assets less liabilities equals owner's equity. If you take a look at your assets and subtract your debts you'll see your equity, or net worth. On paper this is initially disappointing for college students because your biggest asset is your college diploma and your ability to earn income in future decades and there isn't a reliable way to attach a dollar value to account for it. When we take the equation literally and subtract your student loan debt from the resale value of your material goods, perhaps including a used car, you're going to get a negative number. We can't assume that the college degree is worth exactly what you paid for it. First off, starting salaries make certain majors appear more valuable than others, although the financial cost of those degrees is the same. Look at how many CEOs historically have those initially low-value English or philosophy degrees, and the picture gets more complicated. Unlike most every material good you buy, which loses value the minute you take it home (going from new to used in an instant), your degree pays off over years, but that payoff is dependent on so many other considerations: your major, your network, your lucky breaks, where you live while using the degree, and how the world changes over the next 30–40 years. That said, it's worth something, so your true balance sheet does actually have some owner's equity—as long as you finish that degree.

The other key document for an organization is the profit and loss statement, which looks at a range of time and subtracts expenses from revenues to yield net income. Net income is a concept you should very simply see in play with all your campus extracurriculars. Clubs, teams, plays, concerts, fundraisers, radio stations, and journals all have to break even to survive. Your sorority, the outdoor club, and the beekeeping club cannot run a negative net income. They have no ability to borrow, so their books must always balance. In fact, typically, they need to run a little bit of a profit in a given year so they have money to carry over into the next event or year. When you can't borrow to cover a deficit, you simply cannot run a deficit. While the press coverage of venture capital–funded social media or app-developing startups might lead you to believe that organizations can lose hundreds of millions without feeling any pain, even they have concerns about their cash burn rates.

There is no scenario where your future career won't involve an organization trying to live within its means. Knowing what to do when you're about to go over budget, either because your earnings aren't coming in as planned or because expenses are running too high, will always be a valuable experience. Even if you never have direct control over revenue or expenses, anticipating the possible outcome of a slowdown with your employer will give you a running start on your own next move.

The generic solution is simple: find a way to not lose money. The specific solution for your group in that moment will always be more complicated, as is your own budget, but you've got to find a way to make net income stay positive.

The more you borrow from next year's budget, the bigger the hole you are digging. Keep this in mind as you look at solutions, and you'll be able to make the best of a series of undesirable choices. It's far better for the outdoor club to scale down the number of excursions this spring, for your fraternity to cancel the annual spring road trip, for you to deactivate from the sorority, or sit out the optional spring break trip, than it is to make the group or your own net income number go negative. We can never predict the future, and borrowing because your group is counting on a winning vote to raise dues, a bigger budget from the administration, or a bumper crop of honey to sell at homecoming weekend is a dangerous game.

By the same token, while going negative for a reasonable amount of student loan debt in order to get your degree might be an excellent decision, going into debt for a social life or a fancier car or apartment than you can actually afford is always a bad decision. The perfect summer internship for your dream career may turn out to be unpaid, and you'll need a buffer to carry you through. Your reliable Honda may need an unexpected and expensive repair. If that repair needs to go on a credit card so you can get to school or work, then it may be a good investment, but if your credit card is maxed out from the spring break of a lifetime last month with your cast mates from the Shakespeare festival, you're putting your entire future at risk. Plan for the best-case scenario, but always have a buffer. If money is tight for you all through college, live like money is tight. I assure you, that's the case for most students and their parents. The important thing is to get the degree, the experience, and the skills to launch into your chosen career, while minimizing how negative your net income statement is for this time period.

In my case, the fact that my parents paid for UCLA in full (when it was a fraction of the current cost), then largely covered my MBA expenses after I had worked for a couple of years, and that my husband had gone to Whitman College on an academic scholarship, meant that we had little debt as young adults. When we had the idea to start our business that absence of debt and a relatively low-expense lifestyle were what let us sequentially forgo full-time employment and launch a business.

RELATE

While I'm sure it feels like all of your experiences involve relating to people, one of the biggest gripes from employers is a lack of communication and interpersonal skills. A survey by the Workforce Solutions Group noted that over 60 percent of applicants are lacking in this area. If you look around, you will be hard-pressed to identify the 60 percent of your peers who are failing, so consider perhaps that the interpersonal skills that college social and academic life requires are not the same as those required to be successful in a career. All the empirical evidence keeps coming back to this point, and further underlining the problem is that students don't see the deficit. They report confidence in their skills with double-digit differences between their opinions and those of managers working with new graduates. The problem here is that workplace norms may differ between companies, but they all differ quite significantly from your social and academic roles. It's impossible to know exactly what you don't know and very easy to miss all the signals. Unlike your social and academic milieus, the wrong turns won't be called out. While a social group may groan or remain silent when faced with a faux pas and a professor will respond fairly promptly with graded feedback, most jobs provide little feedback and none of it is immediate. Once your reputation goes bad, even a 30-day review is too little, too late for you to substantially change people's opinion of you.

For example, you might be quite charming with a booming social life while being the last person your friends would count on in a pinch. In a work environment, that's really all there is. In a social setting with your parents' friends, perhaps it would occur to you to offer to help your hostess carry out food, resupply chips, or do the dishes. In work, you may not know how to help when not specifically tasked to do so, but the failure to be busy will establish your reputation in a negative way when everyone else is swamped. Merely staying out of the way is rarely a good thing for your career.

In your academic career your professors grade you on your work. In a great school with small classes and very engaged professors, perhaps they will encourage you to speak up more or come to office hours for more specific feedback, but grades are seen as a reflection of the student's work, not the teacher's. That scenario doesn't create any incentive for them to groom the disengaged. If you are 10 minutes late to class, but getting 95 percent on the tests, then you'll get an A, while that chronic lateness in a work environment will very rarely be acceptable even in an otherwise star performer.

As you go looking for groups to get involved with on campus, there are things you can do to test your interoffice people skills, flushing out the weaknesses and finding ways to improve before your job is at stake. The main considerations should be looking for different groups, both in terms of their styles and their life cycle stage as well as with an eye to diversity. Every organization is full of different tribes of people—banded together by common backgrounds, interests, or activities—and the more experience you have dealing with differing tribes, different opinions, and people with different levels of power within a given group, the better you will be able to succeed in an office stratified not only by peers, subordinates, and managers, but all their different subgroups of interests and backgrounds. And the more time you spend with different groups, the better you will be at quickly recognizing the hallmarks of workplaces where you will thrive.

GROUPS ON CAMPUS

Create a Group

Joining a group that is just starting out, whether you are the founder or just jumping on board at the outset, is a unique situation. Admissions tours love to boast about all the existing clubs on campus and are always willing to talk about the newest start-ups. There's a practical catch to that statement, which is why they don't have even more groups on campus. Once you decide to start a group, you need to recruit other members. That's a special skill, and with hundreds of groups on campus, most obvious niches with critical mass have been filled in past years. It's a lot of work. You'll need a high tolerance for chaos and changes in direction, and have to be willing to wear a lot of hats to help build a sustainable organization. Managing all that while also building a whole new life on campus freshman year is a daunting task, but it may be something you still want to pursue.

If you are a passionate birdwatcher who has left behind a treasured family, neighborhood, or school group that shared your passion, you absolutely should try and recreate that happy space for yourself in your new home. Does your school require official organization status to post fliers or book meeting spaces or only to access funding? Most colleges have a very simple process to get a new extracurricular group funded, but timing may vary and perhaps funds are tight, so proof of concept will make that application stronger when the cycle opens up again. **Don't give up.** If you want a group to exist, odds are other people do, too. And finding new friends is always worth a lot of effort. Who's your logical constituency? It's likely the Biology department has some professors, TAs, or staff who are birdwatchers. What about local groups like the Audubon Society? Or online resources for local birding hot spots? Just like a business with a new product, you need to have a plan to approach your logical first customers (the low-hanging fruit). Once you have a few members, they'll tap into their resources and growing the group may be organic from that point forward. Some groups may require more regimented processes for selecting members, when talent is required and the space is limited, as with a barbershop quartet. At what point does it harm the group to have a completely open admissions policy? Is there a way to expand that, to replicate? You pay that student activity fee, as does every other student on campus—even graduate students. Make sure that you get to use your share of those funds, even if it takes some extra effort.

When I first visited Denison University with my son, Jake, I heard there were four different a cappella singing groups on campus. One male, one female, and two coed, with one focused on gospel music. While I don't know the origin stories for these groups, I do know the all-male group is the oldest, so it's easy to imagine that the other groups would naturally have been created over time to meet other a cappella student performers' needs. Learning how to create a new group with no set rules to guide the decision process and finding compromises that work for the group is a unique chance to practice leading people and building a constituency of supporters. You can imagine that when a coed or female group of singers approached the administration about starting a new group, it was a fairly easy case to make—the school is attracting these talents and the all-male group isn't meeting all the needs of the student body. A female, coed, and coed gospel group, in whatever order they came into being, all had a clear differentiator from the others groups in existence. Despite our family having no chance of producing a singer for these groups, seeing all of them perform in the crucial senior year April decision visit gave me a great sense of the talented, inclusive, funny, and charming type of diverse students Denison attracts, making the school itself the richer for supporting so many different groups. While the specifics were irrelevant to our family, the impression made it easy to back Jake's decision, arrived at through his own process. I can retroactively write the proposals in my head for each of those groups, and would bet all were quickly approved, funded, and promoted.

Recruit People

Recruiting people helps you with your sales skills, or course, and helps refine the group's growth. For your group to survive and stay focused, you'll need people with different skills, different networks, yet similar goals. The process of recruiting new people to a new group will demand you develop a simple, straightforward pitch for the group. Being honest and transparent lets you provide more information to more parties who might be able to help reach your goals. Most thriving organizations value transparency because there's recognition that all the different viewpoints within a company can help field test ideas much earlier in the process of developing services, products, or even something as simple as a new form. To cultivate transparency, you need to be the kind of person who recruits and encourages new voices, who is willing to hear new ideas, and is open to hearing about the flaws in your thinking. You need to see the impact your decisions have on the group as a whole. Building out your group's talent pool will enable you to encounter objections and get comfortable with hearing constructive criticism. You'll learn to hear what is being said, but also to read people and get a feel for what's not being said out loud.

Given that the workplace is always going to be slow to give the kind of fast feedback you are used to socially and academically, developing a comfort with soliciting offline feedback from your coworkers and managers will further accelerate your career. Soliciting small amounts of feedback in a casual way without seeming like a needy, insecure middle schooler takes practice, and this kind of beta testing will naturally arise as you create a new group on campus. As you make plans, you'll get market feedback in seeing members honor their commitment and new people wanting to join the group. I'm not advocating for a large-sized group, if that's not appropriate. As long as your group is large enough to function and carry the workload you've set for yourselves, then it's a healthy group.

Some groups may be deliberately impermanent. Perhaps you've finally hit the stage in your college career where a class is so challenging that you need a study group. The same skills go into making a semester-long group. There may be one outlier whose schedule just doesn't mesh with everyone else's willingness to compromise and you may be the person who has to break that news. Even if you think it would be useful to keep a group together all through college, say a weekly dinner for French majors and minors who plan to go abroad junior year, I'd recommend that you set it up as a shorter-term commitment. Seeing who can show up regularly for a semester's worth of dinners and is committed to speaking only French for two hours, or which native speakers are kind to the beginners in the group ,would all be great things to determine in a research stage. You could then go back to a smaller subset of the group at the end of the semester and create a variation on the group. Even the most dedicated, including you, may find as your time in college progresses that interests change. Honoring your top priorities can require hard decisions. I write in more detail in the "Execute" section about knowing when to leave a group yourself. I do want to call out that part of building relationships and a good working team is being understanding when *other* people need to leave. If they can't quite figure that out on their own, you may even find you have to nudge them out the door for the health of the group.

Grow a Group

Once your group is up and running, in your remaining years in college or the community, you can set about growing the organization. Whether you just need to replace the guys in the quartet as they graduate or you need to meet an organizational minimum with each mock trial team having at least six, but not more than 10 students, you can still expand the work of the group by increasing the number of performances or competitions. If you start with one camping trip per semester, try to move to two. It's not growth just for growth's sake, but to see how the complexity expands with more moving pieces. As the organization takes on more commitments you'll need more infrastructure, people, and money. That all adds up to more planning on your part, more testing the system until it breaks. I hope you can embrace the idea that failing now is a good thing, not a bad thing. Effectively college is the beta test stage of your life (or one of them) and you want to flush out the bugs, gaining insight into how people work together when the unexpected happens, developing a working prototype over time.

If your passions have led you to well-established campus or community groups, there's still opportunity to improve. For example, most religious groups on campus are going to be established and the membership will naturally be those students who share your faith and want to actively be involved in the faith community. Colleges also tend to have significant interfaith councils getting all those groups to work together. This means that there's no need to actively grow your membership and no room to invent new religious celebrations. Perhaps your group can find other ways to interact. Any faith-based group will focus on helping those less fortunate, so the way to grow at your school might be to replace a monthly lecture with a service-based activity focused on the larger community. Perhaps the campus group for meditation could start an open class or bring in a lecturer to talk about recent developments in research that reinforce the value of a daily mindfulness practice. The event can be a one-time only experiment. If successful, you can decide if it might be worth repeating annually, quarterly, or monthly. And perhaps it's a great event, and while you don't have the time to take it up a level, there are others who might be willing to take it over. You'll learn things doing something for the first time, and other things if you keep it going, and still other lessons will be gleaned in handing it off to other people and walking away.

Leave a Legacy

One of the most challenging things for successful people to do in all areas of their lives is to delegate. If you care intensely about a project and develop a set of systems that work for you to run the project, it can be very hard to delegate portions of the work. It can be nearly impossible to imagine that you might have to hand the entire project over to someone new. The beauty of the college experience is that is a finite time in your life. You will eventually move on to a new stage of life. You do get promoted each year, which requires that you take on new commitments and give up some old ones to free up time for the new. The same thing will happen in your career, although over a longer time frame. No matter how much you love any given job or position, the goal is certainly to be promoted—to get more responsibilities, to do things that are more valuable, and to be compensated accordingly. Whether you move to a new department, a new company, or a new city, those former bosses and colleagues become your references for the job after this one. Even while you're working with them, being a shining star, you will get sick and go on vacation. If only for this self-interested, reputation-protecting reason, you need to be sure that they think well of you while you're on vacation and after you've gone for good. The fastest way to irredeemably destroy your golden reputation is to leave no road map for the next person to do your job. The fact that it falls apart after you leave will never be viewed as a testament to how amazing you are. It will be viewed as a failure on your part.

In college you will have many opportunities to build systems for projects you undertake. These should be built with an eye to what it's like for someone else to take over the workload. Ideally, your organizations have a succession plan. A sorority vice president is presumably doing her VP job while also watching the current president, knowing that the following year, that's the job she'll be taking on. Many volunteer boards limit terms to two years in order to ensure that they don't have the same treasurer or president for eight successive years. While it's great to have that dedicated volunteer, if they do one job for many years, the organization will lose the broader base of institutional knowledge. If the dedicated volunteer steps down suddenly because of health or geographic issues, their predecessor is long gone, and all knowledge can be lost. As you do a given job, document your work with an eye to leaving a set of notes. Think from the very start about how you would pass the job on. What would happen if you vanished one day? Would the event have to be canceled? Would the campus group have to fold? None of these are good outcomes for the campus or for your reputation.

There are a few basic rules to creating a succession plan. Create free position-based email addresses that you can pass on to your replacement. If the college can't provide these, create accounts on Gmail or a similar free platform. This keeps information out of your personal email and in an easy account you can hand off to someone new. When they inherit the email address, it comes with the archived or filed old emails, eventually covering years of effort. Make sure there are centralized records. Whether your group has a mailing list in email or for USPS, make sure that information is in a shareable platform. Make a free Dropbox account or use the Google Drive associated with the Gmail account. Be sure a couple of trusted people have the passwords to these accounts. If your organization is working outside the school's official boundaries for some reason, open a separate checking account for the group, and put more than one person on that account (any two or three unrelated people can have a joint account). Don't ever mingle the group's funds with your own—it's a bad precedent. Even cash earned in a casual car wash or bake sale fundraiser setting is best set up with another person signing a note that you started the morning with the cash box stocked with $40 in change contributed from your personal funds. At the end of the event, they can then pay you back your original loan and destroy the IOU note. You may be incredibly honest, but that doesn't mean that everyone who ever holds the job will be as resistant to temptation, so it's best to set up good practices from the start. Note these as official procedures in your detailed road map and no one will ever be in the awkward position of demanding that these new rules NOW need to be instituted or ever seen doing something that looks strange to someone who doesn't know the full story.

Staff your group or event with several people and determine who might have the interest or skills to take on more in the future.

Develop that talent. Ideally your senior year you should be an advisor, no longer doing a large portion of the work. Only in this fashion can you set the group up to succeed after your leave.

In a work environment, it will likely be many years before you are asked to develop new talent and train your successor. But having the skills to find and train temps, interns, or newly hired peers as a result of your college experience means that you can create opportunities at work or as a volunteer in which you will be seen as a person who can not only do the work well, but manage other people. That will make you more valuable, more quickly. When other people have to step in and cover your work because you are out sick or on vacation and they find a logical, clear trail to follow, your reputation as a team player and strategic thinker will be reinforced.

In my experience with designers and film editors, the real test of someone's work isn't how the finished project looks, it's how the file looks when we open it up to make an edit. It is not unusual for us to get a rush request for a change to a completed project. Whether there's been a last-minute trademark change on a new project or a sudden staffing change requiring a corporate overview video from two years ago quickly have a clip pulled, typically those requests come in outside of working hours. When we're reopening a file, the hidden quality of someone's work is readily apparent. With a print project built in Adobe InDesign, seeing overflow type warnings (even when it's just excess returns), extraneous boxes with no reason for existing, spaces replacing tabs, paragraphs of copy that look good, but weren't built with style sheets so they fall apart when a word is inserted or removed, are all telltale signs that the attention to detail isn't up to our standard. And those things do matter, because making one quick change suddenly becomes a major job of fixing an untrustworthy file. And that untrustworthy file can make your work a little suspect. It can change what projects you get assigned in the future. With student projects in film editing, it's easy to throw everything into one place because you know you can find it and you understand the method to your madness. But in a work environment, other people have to jump into your files all the time. Maybe you're out, maybe it's a new project where the animation you built in After Effects in English now has to be redone in Chinese. When the next person opens that file there should be a clear folder and composition structure that shows which things are current and which are unused experiments or earlier revisions. It should be obvious where to start working and where to look for older information. Think about your project and event files in any software or cloud account the same way. Organize them by year or by subject or job. Discuss your plan with someone else to get their feedback on the proposed system. Another lesson learned over the course of my career is that no file should ever be named "final"—there will often be a need for a final2, or final3. It's much better to date the revisions or label them rev1, rev2—anything that will let a reasonable person determine that rev9 or the one with the latest date is clearly the final file. It is also really helpful to stash old versions in a folder labeled "old versions 2015 bake sale". The old documents can be really useful, just not mixed in with the current revisions of materials.

SEEK DIVERSITY

As a part of Denison University's Parent Advancement Council, I was provided with University of Wisconsin-Madison Professor William Cronon's 1998 essay "Only Connect: The Goals of a Liberal Education" from *The American Scholar*. It's a great essay, and should be part of the reading for every high school junior and their family as they begin the college search. Professor Cronin lists the 10 qualities he admires in people who embody the values of a liberal education. If you're familiar with the essay, you're probably thinking I'm going to write about number eight (They understand how to get things done in the world), but it's actually a line in his seventh quality that I want to highlight here, "They have the intellectual range and emotional generosity to step outside their own experiences and prejudices, thereby opening themselves to perspectives different from their own." This is the crux of the problem for students who are focused on leadership roles in only one group.

Move Outside Your Usual Tribe

If all your extracurricular involvement is focused on being the head of your sorority, you're not dealing with a diverse group. You've all self-selected to be in the house. Each rush week the existing members vote which incoming members to take, and you're all bound by a set of rules about behaviors from dues to attire for key events to chapter meetings. You are mostly from families that can afford the extra expense of dues and the required attire and you probably share a lot of the same cultural values. The real world isn't going to be like that. Your teams of coworkers are going to be a much more mixed group, and the people in meetings are going to have different skills and different agendas. Some people will be in meetings who don't want to be there at all and you're going to have to hold their attention. Don't get me wrong, running a meeting—having an agenda, staying on schedule, getting through sorority business—it's all valuable. But be sure you're looking at other opportunities, too. Work for the newspaper, join a different club, or better yet, have your sorority work to advance the goals of another group. Team up with the outdoor club to do something, whether it's a fundraiser or a social event. Too often sororities and fraternities only team up with other Greek organizations on campus. All that cooperation is probably great for their social lives, but less valuable for managing a diversity of opinions, values, priorities, and goals.

Seek Out Different Opinions and Agendas

As I'm sure you've noticed, most human beings like to cling to their world views which frequently involve an "us versus them" stance. An exploitive business may even have this view of its customers. Certainly all businesses tend to view the competition as outsiders. But flipping that paradigm and assuming there's value in the other side's viewpoint is a great way to get competitive intelligence. In what ways are they great? Can you incorporate some of their strong points without trying to be all things to all people? Microsoft was the business standard, so Apple staked out the hip side of the divide. Apple products may be a reliable and safe choice, but they don't sell on that idea. They claimed the outsider status not only because it fit their attitude but also because when they started it was going to be a hell of a slog to be the safe corporate choice. A business will have a hard time claiming to be both local and global. Some things just don't go together. But businesses constantly look at the competition to see where there might be unexploited opportunities that could be won at a relatively low cost. To do that they need to look at what the competition has missed or is doing wrong, but to execute that strategy they also need to look at what's working in other departments, other countries, and with other groups of customers. Make sure you cultivate that kind of flexibility not only in academic pursuits but in your extracurricular opportunities. In the real world people switch teams, so you'll want to have an open mind about other companies and other industries. The best way to practice that kind of flexibility outside of the classroom is to work with other, different groups on campus.

Campus Democrats and Republicans could easily claim irreconcilable differences based on the example set by their elders, but on campus it should be much clearer that your other teams, clubs, and housing affiliations contain a full range of political parties. They could all work together to register new voters, make sure your freshman men have registered for the (theoretical) draft as required by law, put on a series of debates, or attract politicians to speak on campus. Maybe the LGQBT groups can work with a religious group to raise funds for a local animal shelter. Get the presumably more affluent students on the sailing team working with the first-to-attend-college to arrange a campus-wide trash pickup. Look for common ground with groups where there doesn't seem to be anything obvious.

We can all agree we don't want kittens euthanized, kindergartners falling behind in reading or fitness, that local parks should have more trees, that a community garden is a good idea, that building a home for a family without one is a great use of a weekend. When you find an idea you want to make reality, recruit from outside your circle of friends and coworkers. Fight the stereotypical event pairings. It's not surprising when the Greek system is involved in promoting the big game, but fraternities raising money for an elementary school's library or running bingo once a month for the local retirement community are more outside the box. These kinds of events will keep your mind flexible and open to new ways to relate to other people. The more diverse your experiences, the more naturally willing you will be to recruit marketing's support early on in engineering designs or to ask the Europe, the Middle East, and Africa (EMEA) group to weigh in on a North American advertising campaign. While their expertise may not feed into your customer base, it would be great to have early awareness of how that corporate branding effort might be perceived in other cultures.

Work with Different Levels of Power

Relationships in college will not have the obvious stratification you experienced as a high school student. Some professors, staff, and administrators will be much more flexible than the discipline-focused authority exerted by their K-12 counterparts. The distinctions between the different classes of students lose their power when some newbies come in as transfers, while other freshman have enough Advanced Placement (AP) credit to start as sophomores. Add in off-campus housing and everyone being a legal adult, and there's little visible demarcation in most groups. Work can be much the same, but be forewarned: there is a hierarchy in play even in the most open organizations. Power may be allocated by seniority, department, skills, or something else entirely, but it's always in play—even at our small company, where we welcome input and have changed considerably over the years as a result of the influences of both staff and clients. I've got a pretty good grip on the strategic world view as it applies to our overall business. I've been there for 25 years and am the resident business nerd. I have the anti-zen job: my focus is entirely on the future and the past. The present is perfectly handled by everyone else. I hope I'm open to hearing new things and considering how to apply those ideas. I get a ton of new ideas myself from listening to podcasts and reading. I love change and am always asking myself how we can be better, but I know there are times when I just can't explain all the years of back story behind my unwillingness to consider a particular suggestion. I know I move too fast for some tastes when I'm implementing my newest great idea. Undoubtedly the same is true at least some of the time when you encounter resistance from a faculty advisor or administrator on campus. It may even be as simple as them being overloaded and knowing that a lot of the work to implement the idea will fall to them.

Your campus adventures should provide ample chances to manage up. This is different than manipulating parents into granting permission or teachers into giving you those missing points you feel your essay deserved. Managing up is silly phrase that can take you to dangerous places. The key is that you're not trying to work around those above you in the power structure. You should be looking at where they are strong or weak and how you might supplement their efforts. Look at what their goals are and how you might help facilitate those. Consider their style of working and think about how you might accommodate that. If you can improve their experience of working with you, you'll find that your life also gets easier as you dodge situations that drain your productivity and block your own goals.

Get used to finding a good time to talk to someone higher up on the food chain. Just because it's urgent for you to talk to career services this Friday, if they are hosting their major law school reception, this isn't the best time for you to show up. Take a breath and consider whether this is a good time. Can you get an answer (or help calming down) from another source? Pay attention to the signs other people are giving you. A physics TA coming out of the office with her arms full, scrambling to lock the door is clearly on her way to something else. It may not even be the right time to ask when a good time might be. Since you need to get used to presenting solutions, not problems, use the delay to go off and develop some possible solutions. Even if you're only partway to a solution, it's still a good idea to come to the table with a smaller ask. Make sure higher ups look good. Don't let your faculty advisor get caught out unaware of a major issue with your club. If the outdoor club made a stop at an emergency room on that rafting trip in California over spring break, make sure the relevant parents and school authorities know. Ideally you can all handle it and just let them know when the solution is in hand, but when reporting back won't slow you down unsafely, get a text or call off to them, telling them which student appears to have broken their collarbone, where you are now, and what solution is in process. But if it's 3:00 a.m. back in Iowa, maybe wait and make that call in another three hours, or communicate via email—they'll get the information but not be woken up. When you have to call your boss to say you didn't send the project out as planned, you'll be in much better shape if they saw that coming six hours earlier and have been able to get an extension from the client or add more resources to the project. Rather than praying you make an impossible deadline and emerge a hero, ask for help earlier and make the whole team successful.

Managing your peers can be easier in a group with a clear hierarchy, but at work that power structure may not always be clear. Be sure you welcome the opportunity to deliver the same kind of support to your peers on the team. If you're worried someone is going to miss their deadline and doesn't seem to be communicating with you, reach out and see if you can help. If the reliability of team members on a class project is unknown, set up a milestone calendar with meetings so you're all accountable for the preliminary parts like outlines and drafts, from which the final presentation will flow. Don't patronize or over-direct your peers, but be the person who asks about the process and helps to set up a system that will flush out problems before they are fatal. While the work world is in desperate need of an endless supply of strong coders who don't need much sleep, eight years from now the people who progress in their careers will have done a little less coding in favor of a little more project management. Those skills will not be taught in a class or as part of a training program. You have to cultivate every chance to build a team that excels, so you embed those skills into your working style.

As tempting as it might be in a hierarchical system to lord it over your initiates, this period, always instituted to build a bond among the new group of members, really should deliver on the promise. Merely surviving terrible hazing fails on both fronts. You learn nothing and neither does the incoming group of members. If you can modify those traditions to build a sense of teamwork even in the slightest way, you'll gain real skills both in managing your peers and developing new talent. Any activity that brings them into your group while also getting them to work together to overcome difficulty will bond them to each other and the organization as a whole. In the work world, as new people come on board, whether as new hires or through acquired companies, the faster everyone starts working together, maximizing each other's strengths, the faster the organization reaches its goals. A bad start not only slows down the achievement of those goals but it can drive the acquired talent right out of the company, permanently diluting the company's capability to achieve the projected outcome.

Think about your group's onboarding process. Are you providing new members with the tools they need to be successful within the organization? Are the goals transparent? Do they have the supplies and direction they need to be happy and productive? If your sorority has an expensive social life, full of travel or new formal wear, be sure your potential pledges see that outlay coming. A successful rush has to yield the right number of new members, but they need to be members who can afford to stay active in the group. Admissions works on many of the same principles: every year they want to fill the freshman class and refill any spots that have opened up in the upper grades. But they also want to accept a mix of students who meet their overall goals for the school—the right athletes, performers, chemistry majors, students from all the states, a dozen different countries, and a ton of other population segments. They want to acquire students who not only meet those demographic requirements, but who are also likely to be successful and happy at the school. They want students who can do the work, pay the tuition, contribute to the community, and go on to success (ideally donating money to their beloved alma mater for the rest of their lives). That's why so much thought goes into recruitment, admissions, new student orientation, academic majors, and the amazing array of extracurriculars available to you. Your approach in managing new members should be much simpler but it should consider their motivations and needs as well as the group's. You want them to be happy, fully engaged, and committed. Thinking about how you might create systems falls under the previous Organize section, so in this section I'm not talking about the tactical solution, but rather making sure you're aware of how you're relating to the people around you. The more you can put yourself in someone else's place and consider their agenda, the better able you are to facilitate your own success.

EXECUTE

Execution at the most basic level is delivering on your promises. If you say that you'll be there at 7:00 p.m., then be there at 6:50 p.m. If you say the outdoor club budget will be done on Tuesday, deliver on Monday afternoon. If you say you will do anything, get it done. But also get it done right and early. Whatever you did in high school got you accepted into your college, which probably means you've been doing this for years. A couple of key differences about your new college life make it worth starting this section with basics. A fair amount of students have adults in their lives who made sure these plates all kept spinning. Because you were so busy, and the stakes (seemed to be) so high, it is possible that you had these kinds of adults. Whether parents, teachers, or coaches, if some of your success was due to wake-up calls, reminders, double-checks, or flat-out personal assistant services like packing, typing, travel booking, or calendar-keeping, you need to start doing the full juggle on your own. Every time mom books your plane ticket home, you've missed an opportunity to get used to thinking about how it all fits together. When is your last final? When is the next flight? Do you have time to pack up between those two events or earlier in the week? What comes home for the summer? What goes into storage? How are you getting to the airport? What's your budget for the trip? What's the price of the airline ticket versus the train or bus? Which airline is really cheaper when you consider baggage fees? What's your sister doing? Can you coordinate your flights so you get into the airport at home at the same time so mom can do one pickup? Dad booking that flight doesn't seem like much and you are just so busy, but there's a big trade-off in giving up these opportunities to think about the bigger picture.

Follow Through

While all classes require you commit and deliver on a basic set of obligations, some classes can provide great practice in complex execution. If your school permits a senior thesis, plan on doing one. Look for interdisciplinary courses, or project-centric electives that require you to look at a big chunk of information, make some assumptions, put forth a theory, and support it. As an English major, I took an upper division class that required each week we read a different eighteenth-century novel and discuss it in class. We had some short writing assignments, but half our grade was the final. Near the end of the 10-week long quarter the professor let us know that the final was to write a paper explaining how all these books were connected. That's all the direction we had and we'd read a total of 10 novels and memoirs. Oh, and the paper had to be between 18 and 20 pages long. It was terrifying and stressful, but once I had a thesis, poring over the books and writing my paper was a totally absorbing joy. Good thing I enjoyed it, because the whole rest of my work life has been thousands of projects that have been a variation on that theme.

Even in a basic college class, the point of getting an A isn't the A itself. The real goal is the acquisition of the knowledge, but a more basic class will tie into real work skills when you are doing top-level work. Hand in papers that don't require feedback. They should be free of spelling errors—both those of ignorance and carelessness. They should be free of grammatical errors. It doesn't matter that the professor can figure out what you were trying to say with that equation. It matters that you've specified exactly what you want to a fabricator. In the work world, if you give a weird specification, you'll get the wrong thing back and have to pay good money for it. It's not the job of your boss or a client to intuit what you were saying or fill in the gaps. You might have an amazing vendor who questions something out of line, but it's also not their job to do so. If you had that particular order-processing or fabricating job at the vendor company, you would, I know, question a weird spec and ask for confirmation, but technically and contractually, as a business, it's not their responsibility.

If you require micromanagement in the real world one of two things will happen: you will get it and hate the job or you won't get it and mistakes will happen—whether of commission or omission. Either of these outcomes doesn't put you in line for the increased responsibilities that give you promotions and raises. At the very least you won't be able to learn much or develop better skills. By the same token, as you take on extracurricular positions, be so reliable that you don't get micromanaged by staff. If micromanaged by a peer, do your best to resolve the issue (good practice for dealing with bad bosses) but also be prepared to finish your tour of duty and move on to a different group. As you begin to move up the leadership ranks, be careful you're not a micromanager. There are two problems with being unable to delegate: no one will want to work with you, so you'll get no experience managing a team and no one will be willing or able to take the position over and the organization may not survive your graduation. One of the great things about the four-year cycle of college is that everyone should be rotating through positions, which is much like the world of work. In a work environment people are always coming and going, whether through hiring, leaving, vacations, promotions, family leaves, travel, departmental reassignments, or promotions.

Micromanagement is exactly as annoying as it was in your preteen years when your parents were still doing things you wanted to do for yourself. It probably pushes the same childhood buttons for most people. Every parent eventually has to stop brushing their young child's teeth and let the child do it, even when they know the child isn't as good at brushing as the parent and the consequences of that subpar performance are both permanent physical damage and short-term expense. The same thought process applies to the parts of your job. If you think you are the only one who can book the venue, write and design the program, sell the tickets, decorate the entry, and clean up after the show, you are micromanaging other people. In any college activity, a productive timeline would be to spend a year participating and helping, maybe another year assisting the person running a component of the event, a year running it yourself with someone assisting or following you, and a year being available to help your protégé succeed. Even if you create the club or event out of thin air, the idea should be to organize and recruit others with skills stronger than yours to help with some areas.

Keep an eye on the skills you need. Focus on new skills you should gain, even if they aren't comfortable. Remember, failing now with a supportive team around you is pretty painless. And the reality is you'll all feel so comfortable working together that neither the staff nor your peers will let you fail. If that freshman completely screws up the program your junior year, you're going to step in and coach her, or even stay up all night to redo it yourself, right? Everyone else is going to provide you and the group the same level of support if you can't get the budget to balance your second year. Communicating the roadblocks in a timely manner is part of the learning experience. Even if you are a studio art major who wants to be a graphic designer you still don't need to do the posters and program for a campus-wide event for more than a year or two. You also need the experience of lobbying the administration, presenting the proposal, managing other people, organizing parts of the event, selling tickets, and watching the budget.

Many campuses now host TEDx events, and any community group is welcome to set one up. The TED.com website does a great job of walking a potential organizer through what's needed to create a compelling event and stay true to their mission of presenting "Ideas Worth Spreading". Even if you have no interest in TED talks or that scope seems way too large for your current skills, take advantage of these kinds of websites—reviewing their planning process can ensure your planning process isn't missing any key steps. Remember, some failure is to be expected. Putting on an event that flops or just doesn't seem to have the support required to repeat on an annual basis is a completely acceptable outcome. The process of *trying*, not achieving a perfect outcome, builds your skills. You're not starting a new business, no one is betting their life savings, people aren't counting on recurring revenue to pay their rent. All of this means you are free to experiment. If you put on an event that works well one month or one year and flops the second, solicit feedback on how it could have succeeded. College can serve as a laboratory for an infinite number of experiments on how to make a plan, improve a plan, and execute a plan. You just have to keep looking for chances to try this out.

If the original idea is what escapes you, look around for groups that seem to be addressing worthy issues on campus and see if they are interested in tackling something. Unfortunately a lot of people find a group of like-minded people and create a list of demands—and have no interest in making the kind of compromises it takes to agree on objectives and tackle possible solutions. Perfect is truly the enemy of done. While recycling doesn't stop global warming it's still worthwhile. Small changes in behavior can shift community mores, change how people see themselves, and begin to shift the overall conversation. Over time, these kinds of small shifts can be transformative for a community. In the short run they are always transformative for the people who work on them. Getting a group together to raise $2,000 to provide one-time, emergency $50 grants to freshman students in need could begin a conversation about raising more funds for scholarships or loan forgiveness. And if it doesn't do anything more, there would still be a number of students in one academic year who were spared considerable stress and unhappiness because of your work on the project.

Apply Your Technical Skills

Many of the most relevant skills for a given career won't be taught in school, no matter where you go. In many jobs you'll be implementing tools you've learned in classes, but in classes, you'll just be deploying those tools, which isn't the same thing at all. In years of interviewing new graphic designers, I frequently saw beautiful portfolio pieces. The problem was that the work was too conceptual. An assignment that asks students to develop packaging for a new line of children's blocks or organic eggs gives them too much range to generate portfolio pieces that will actually help them get hired. It will be years before they are hired to do work on a blank slate like that. The projects a new graphic designer will tackle require working in a very tightly defined existing brand, so class assignments that involve making a data sheet for a brand extension or packaging for a vegetarian, gluten-free Happy Meal would be more to the point. These are creative and different ideas but related to the existing brand. I think colleges are right in assigning wide-ranging, blank slate projects—it's not like most people go back to school after working for eight years. My point is that taking on projects that do work on a more narrow scope is incredibly valuable. I'd like to see mind-blowing creative, sure. An interview can tell me if a prospective applicant knows how to dress for work, think and speak on their feet, and present their work. But we'd also like some evidence a new designer can happily work under brand guidelines. That they will be willing, able, and happy developing good-looking, utilitarian pieces that fit as part of a larger set. Because sometimes in the real world, the copy for a data sheet is a little longer than it should be, or the chart for the sixth product is 25 percent longer than earlier product brochures. Or the art needs to work in eight languages. A class that drilled you in this might be a little boring, or a little too easy for all the money colleges charge. But if you volunteer to do some work for a local nonprofit, they are going to need a poster, and they might need it in more than one language, and you have to work around the logo they developed three years ago, which has a really difficult shade of purple. The audition posters for mock trial probably should include the college logo. You're going to have to find out who has the official college logo files in a format you can use for a clean print. And acquiring that logo means someone at the school is going to let you know about their official approval process. This is all great news. Because this is exactly what a real job is like, and the more you learn how to go get this information and work through an approval process, the more valuable you are the first day of an internship, much less in a job. And if you've already encountered this kind of process, you will learn so much more in an internship—you have context to understand what you're witnessing. (This is why MBA programs much prefer their applicants have at least a few years in the workplace before they come back to business school.) Mock trial is a serious group, likely largely future lawyers, so they might well have a committee deciding on the poster. You'll need to show them three options for their poster. They'll like the type on one, the layout of two and perhaps the image from option three. So you're either going to have to make that Frankenstein's monster version of the poster or convince them it won't work and that each option one through three already addresses their needs as-is. Alternatively, maybe you can find a design compromise by asking why they feel the way they do. And while we're at it, having successfully delivered a poster, seen them go through the auditions (which some other student, if not you, should have attended and photographed so you have art for next year), go ahead and pitch them a website. Every club needs a basic website, maybe with an embedded calendar. Go find an aspiring programmer and a writer and get going. That's a portfolio item that has an epic story behind it. It may, as work by committees sometimes are, be less beautiful, but the story and the skills of assembling a team, working with a client, and delivering functional work on a timeline and budget is the most valuable thing you'll be showing. It's almost impossible to show portfolio pieces that let you answer interview questions in a way that demonstrates your work ethic, persistence, and client management skills.

Track Your Results

In *The Start-Up of You*, Reid Hoffman and Ben Casnocha perfectly articulate the need to develop a competitive advantage, specifically noting "people list impressive-sounding-yet-vague statements like 'I have two years of experience working at a marketing firm...' instead of specifying, explicitly and clearly, what they're able to do because of those two years of experience." You're going to have this same problem as you develop a résumé, so you not only need to say you did something besides go to school and socialize, but you need to be sure you can point to real results. Failure in this context is fine, if you can explain what you learned by failing. If you ran an outside concert that failed due to a fluke rain storm, then what did you change for next year? Did you presell tickets, set up side events in smaller campus venues, have tent rentals secured months in advance—that you could cancel with limited penalty when the three-day weather forecast looked safe? Solicit feedback as you go. Every time you present, go back to the professor and get feedback. If you present at a science symposium on campus, arrange to have someone film it or to have a professor or even someone from career services attend just to give you presentation (as opposed to science) feedback.

Think about the results as you finish each project, not just at the end of the year (or junior year as you start to interview). While you're compiling some concrete results, you'll also be able to think about what strengths you can build on and address any truly critical weaknesses. Informational interviews can be really helpful with this self-assessment. After finding out about the person's career and soliciting their advice on key skills needed to be successful, always ask if there are any opportunities they wish they'd pursued in college that would have helped them get those skills. If you think their field is a good fit in some ways and still wonder about others, tailor your final questions that direction. Ask if it would be okay to follow up with your résumé or LinkedIn profile in order for them to give you feedback about where it was strong, and what weaknesses they would see in you as an intern or job applicant in their field, so you can address them long before you're in the intern or job market.

Know How and When to Quit

Never give up—*unless of course you really should*. In discussing the execution of plans, we have to talk about the fact that some schools, jobs, relationships, and organizations should be left. There are no prizes in life for playing through either an injury or a lightning storm. Leaving is a tough objective for most people and the younger you are in life, the less likely you are to have ever had to do this. Even if you have had to do this, you may not feel confident you did it well or that you've seen it modeled. This is your life and you shouldn't be doing anything that makes you really unhappy. If it's a bad match or has become a bad match, you need to think about why, see if there's a way to fix it, and then, if there isn't, you need to leave.

There will always be some things that aren't a match, for whatever reason. I've had a dog pretty consistently since third grade, even for a year in college (yep, mom and dad ended up with that dog for the next decade), but when my husband and I adopted a Labrador puppy when our oldest son was a year old, it was a disaster. We both worked, business was booming, we had a house and a child, and had zero time to reinforce all the training required with a puppy. A year into the process (and at least a thousand dollars of property damage later) it was pretty clear I wasn't equipped to be a dog person right then. By the time I was pregnant with our second son, racing from work to pick up a toddler, pulling over to throw up from "morning" sickness every couple of miles on the drive home, we'd hit our limit. We posted a notice at the vet's and happily gave our expensive purebred puppy to a lovely family with three teenagers (who, by the way, had given away a dog under similar circumstances 15 years earlier). I'm still a dog person with a long history of great, super well-trained dogs—but twice in my life I adopted a great dog and it was a terrible mistake for that moment in my life, so I had to find a solution that didn't involve living with the mistake in the service of some outdated and unrealistic idea of who I was.

A group's culture can go bad a lot of ways. There are toxic cultures, where there's actively, aggressively unkind (or illegal) stuff going on treated as unremarkable behavior. There's bullying and hazing. People stealing ideas, sabotaging other people's efforts, or being blind to the larger picture. It can be as simple as recognizing that you're not comfortable with the way a group discusses non-members or as overt as racism, sexism, or dangerous behavior. If you're in a group like this, you need to exit as soon as possible, albeit with some grace.

You don't have to enter the workforce to encounter a bad culture within a group, it's on even the most idyllic campus. Hazing isn't just for the Greek system—other groups can be just as nasty in their rituals, nor are all fraternities guilty of this. Part of college is figuring out who you are and what you stand for. (There is more to these four years than getting a job—a really great school is going to help you learn how to make a life.) You're going to get a lot to think about in the discussion of big ideas in the classroom and during office hours, but you should also be getting it in your non-academic engagements. It's perfectly normal to join a fraternity and decide later that it's not a fit for you. You should change a lot between freshman year rush and senior year grad school applications. By the same token, you may have passed on a sorority freshman year and then find junior year that you have a lot of friends in one who really would love to have you join. And it's never too late to try singing or acting—go try out, if that holds appeal for you. This time in your life is exactly the right time to try new things. If the finances work for you, go for it. As Ralph Waldo Emerson wrote, "A foolish consistency is the hobgoblin of little minds, adored by little statesmen and philosophers and divines."

You can also take a job or internship and find it doesn't work for you—either the place or the whole career path. If you've got an internship, it's probably eight to ten weeks long, so you're going to need to stick it out for the sake of the reference and maybe your résumé. (If you're unpaid and it's a total joke, you can say you need to get a paying job and bail out—though I'd give them the usual two weeks notice if possible.) If it's a bad part-time job, you owe them two weeks notice and little more. If it's your first or second real j ob, they probably figure they've got you for 12 to 24 months, but if it's a disaster, you can safely leave after six months without torching any bridges.

If it's a slightly bad culture, where most people are disengaged, then you'll see simple things going wrong. Look for people who don't work together effectively, do the bare minimum, don't step up to help each other, or wait for work to be assigned (rather than volunteering). There's just not a sense of excitement or any drive towards common goals. People disappear for hours, lunches are long, at quitting time it's as though an invisible factory whistle just blew. You'll see this at school, too. If people (professors or students) bail out of classes (and campus) every time they can, cutting classes is endemic, and there's no sense of community on the weekends, you need to think about transferring (if you're still in freshman or sophomore year). The people at a community college are engaged in a lot of other aspects of their lives so expect those hallmarks of disengagement much less harshly there. Those communities have a lot of part-timers, people juggling work and school, retirees exploring new passions, or professionals picking up additional certifications. It's called community college because it fits into the existing community, not because it is the central hub of a community. That might be a great fit for you as you work to knock out your general ed requirements at a lower price point. Just make sure your target transfer school is the hub of a community, so you get to experience that culture, too.

The main reason to always leave gracefully is the simple logistics of lifetime job hunting. Even when you find the perfect job, you will eventually need to move again to gain new skills, get a big raise, or shorten your commute. You'll have to conduct the hunt for this third job without telling the second job (you can't know how long the hunt will take, and you don't want them firing you or shortchanging your opportunities because they know you are looking). When the potential third job employers want to check references, you'll likely have to give them names from the job before your current position—the first (bad) job. Uh-oh. It never hurts to leave gracefully—leave the way you'd like to be left: firmly, inexorably, but with kindness.

CONCLUSION: BE BRAVE

The time and energy you put into figuring out who you are, what you're good at, and what interests you become part of the biggest asset you may ever acquire. That process accelerates in a big way as you start college. The way we build identity capital, the collection of skills and experiences that make us valuable, is through doing things. We earn this kind of capital via the things we try, the people we meet, the lessons we learn, and the things we accomplish. This is a unique moment in your life—you get a clean slate, you get to start over where hardly anyone knows you, out from under the watchful eyes of your parents. This is a chance to try out a lot of different ways of being, even if your parents swear they are only paying your tuition if you major in computer science.

Even though graduation seems many years away, it will be senior year all too quickly. Aside from the excitement of starting that segment of your life, the financial reality is that you'll want to launch quickly and successfully when the stakes suddenly get that much higher. A successful launch pays off in the short-term economics of collecting a first salaried paycheck faster, but more importantly in the long-term economics of making more money earlier in your career while getting the chance to do more and higher level projects. That kind of success pays off in your happiness doing work that matters to you and having options to change directions as needed.

My hope in writing *Launch Like A Rocket* was to point out a way to strategically bridge the gap between academic and career success. New college graduates want to be seen by their managers as they see themselves: competent, skilled, motivated, and smart. And you absolutely can acquire all those soft skills simply by choosing how you're tackling your college life. As you take on extracurricular activities that interest you, try new things, and risk failure (repeatedly) while the costs are low. I encourage you to get a little out of your comfort zone and push yourself a bit once in awhile. Do all the same things you are already doing—just be sure your decisions are consciously made with a small nod to the needs of your future and an eye to an outsider's view of your overall skills. That small adjustment in choosing how you spend your time can help you get completely ready for real life while you're still in college. I encourage you to prioritize the demands on your time and budget. I encourage you to be kind to yourself—and everyone else. You should work really hard to build a foundation for your future, while also enjoying the current place and people around you.

By involving yourself in extracurricular activities, off-campus jobs, and community volunteering, you not only gain real-world soft skills, but you expand that group of people you interact with to include already-successful adults. The more engaged you are and the stronger your roots in your community, the happier you will be. You should love these activities when you are doing them, but remember they are booster rockets, meant to be shed once they've helped you break out of college's atmosphere, into the great universe beyond.

Research going back to 1973 on the strength of weak ties shows that the people who are really going to help you find a job are the ones with whom you have a weaker association. The people who you know the very best tend to know the exact same things you know. Your fraternity brothers are going to recommend career services, those two alumni from 2010, and the one mom they've all approached for internships and jobs. But that local high school teacher who led the fundraiser for the animal shelter or the alumni board member who worked with you on the homecoming weekend speaker panel your junior year, not only knows you and can vouch for your abilities, but they have *an entirely different network*. A network that isn't a well-trod path for new grads from your school every year. That's why you want a broad, shallow network to help you line up post-degree opportunities.

According to a 2013 article in Forbes, "Six Ways to Crack the Hidden Job Market," some studies are now claiming 80 percent of all jobs get filled before they ever get posted. And a lot of that 80 percent is coming from staff referrals. The wider your circle, the more likely you are to be one of those referrals. You have to make it easy for a lucky break to find you.

Ensure you are worth referring, and that all those earlier experiences are building into something real. You need a network, a résumé, and a set of interview talking points that show you to be accomplished, experienced, and an excellent pick for the position you are targeting. Remember, I've created a planning spreadsheet with a vertical axis of the outlined skills and sub-skills I've discussed and a horizontal axis with the questions you should ask yourself before you take on a new obligation as well as the notes you should be taking in real time as you complete those activities. If you implement the spreadsheet (you can find it at LaunchLikeARocket.com/plan), your updated résumé will write itself by the end of each year.

It's important that the work also pay your bills, so pay attention to needs versus wants and don't confuse the two. Minimize the amount of debt you take on every step of the way. Maximize your savings as you are able. Both those habits will permit you to take risks as your life progresses, whether to change careers, go back to graduate school, start a family, follow a dream, start a business, or simply try something new.

Your career path may not be clear, but if you put one foot in front of the other, your winding path will lead somewhere interesting. (Possibly somewhere far more interesting and less crowded than the obvious straight shot on the freeway.) The important thing in the long run is to find work that is meaningful to you. If the work has meaning, it's easy to work hard, ask questions, and engage with the world. Continuing to fully engage and ask questions will provide you with still more opportunities to choose from as time progresses. And those interactions will create an ever-growing network of people who can open other doors. All those things lead to success, if not always great riches. Just be sure to repay the favor as you progress— help the next set of grads find their way into the world as you find yourself capable of doing so.

Be brave!

WHAT CAN PARENTS DO?

Think Strategically During the College Search

Recent research into brain development reports that the teenage brain is truly not done developing until about age 25. And the part that's still growing, the prefrontal cortex, is what helps us control impulsive behavior and plan to achieve our long-term goals. As a result, when teenagers, typically under 18, are considering college or career options, the biggest value parents and other mentoring adults can provide is a strong sense of the longer-term big picture. Think about where your student will have the most opportunities or the lowest cost. No matter where a student goes to school, owing more than a first year's expected salary upon graduation is going to close off options in life, not open them up. Resist the parental arms race for bragging rights and don't show your student schools that you can't afford. Look at how much merit and need-based aid the schools might give your student. If that's not enough, then those schools probably aren't a good fit. And if a four-year experience is financially unrealistic, look at the local community college. In California they have an excellent program to help motivated successful students transfer into the UC system. This is a great way to get a college degree without saddling your teen with insurmountable debts through adulthood.

Be honest about the kind of student you have. Look at the GPA and test score numbers for any potential school. There's no sense having a student get really excited about a school which has a median SAT score 150 points higher than their current score. Yes, they may improve that score and maybe visiting the school will motivate them to study for another round of the SAT. It may also discourage them that they've found the perfect but totally unobtainable school. It's one thing to have a student who wants to date tall, thin blondes who can sing—that's pretty picky—but if they are only willing to date Taylor Swift, it's laughable. And yet parents frequently tackle the college search in such a way that they are effectively suggesting their student settle for a college experience that is nothing less than that overly-specific, very unlikely outcome.

There's no point in even the most fabulous student falling hopelessly in love with schools that are consistently advertising ridiculously low acceptance rates. I'm not saying they shouldn't apply to those schools, just that parents shouldn't feed the love affair. It really is a roll of the dice that they'd get into any one school, no matter how extraordinary the student. Every year Yale rejects students that Harvard accepts, while UCLA rejects students that Stanford accepts. At least one student at your teen's same high school with slightly lesser grades, test scores, and no special athletic or musical ability will be accepted to a school that rejects your clearly more high-performing student. Your older child may be rejected by a school that accepts your younger child the very next year, even though his grades were lower.

Look for schools that will provide the best opportunities for your student. In many cases you may have to make some educated guesses about where your 16-year-old's passions might lead in terms of majors, extracurriculars, and careers. Again, not to insult any teen-aged readers, but given the state of teen brain development, it's much more difficult for them to really understand the consequences of some of their decisions. And no matter how mature or brilliant your teen, odds are they don't really grasp how hard it is to pay off $80,000 in student loan debt as compared to $20,000. As adults managing our own adult budgets of whatever size, we can offer that perspective. Are there opportunities you or other adults they know had to forgo as a result of academic debt? Are there things that were easier for you because of the absence of that debt? Because you stayed close to home? Went far away? Did a semester abroad? There's nothing wrong with putting your thumb on the scale in the evaluation of options when you have real concerns.

In my experience, it makes the most sense to have these honest conversations about your concerns and the variables that you need to see considered in college selection well before applications are due. The applications process is frequently emotionally overwrought and to have all that drama end with the news that you are unable to afford the dream school or unwilling to have them go so far away, play football, major in dance, or live off campus only adds to the trauma of April acceptances and the panicked need to pick a school and commit by May 1. Having that discussion junior year, well before applications are due, makes for a much calmer process. However tough it is to be the bearer of bad news, it's much better to be honest early in the process.

In our family's case, we knew that we needed some merit aid for both sons. Based on our savings and our income we knew we wouldn't be eligible for need-based aid. Because we felt strongly that we had been able to pursue opportunities in our own adult lives in part as a direct result of having very little student loan debt, we didn't want them to borrow anything for their undergraduate degrees. Since we're self-employed, our income can fluctuate considerably from year to year, and we had to assume that there was always a possibility that we might have bad years in the six-year time period we had one or both in college. And clearly, we had to look honestly at the situation for both of our sons when only the oldest was looking at colleges. No parent wants to tell the younger child they goofed and spent all the money on the older child's education. We had a very honest conversation about money with both boys as they looked at schools, and we considered only schools whose average merit aid award would be adequate to cover our needed amount. To ensure that the boys would be likely to receive that average merit aid award, we looked for schools where their test scores would be in the upper quartile. As a rough guide, we figured this should put them in the upper quartile of applicants, and make them desirable prospective students. We also shared a spreadsheet listing the schools, with expected costs, as well as special notes about why these schools were a strong fit for their interests.

Do your homework—small liberal arts colleges with their increased undergraduate access to labs and funded undergraduate research have better per capita rates of sending students into STEM doctoral programs. That opportunity to literally experiment yields great life results in terms of students finding a passion and trying it on for size. Extracurricular and paying jobs during college have to serve the same purpose for those students who don't want to go on to graduate programs. Be sure the schools you think might be worth showing your student have the programs they are interested in, but also have other options. A 16-year-old who wants to major in biology to go to medical school might end up a doctor, but they may also decide they want to major in engineering. A friend, sibling, or romantic partner may not get in or stay at the school—even if the romance is still going strong by the time they are moving into college. Look for compromises—are there other schools nearby that might be a better fit and yet permit the relationship to continue? A student athlete may or may not be recruited or even want to continue playing their sport at a collegiate level by the time senior year of high school comes. Picking a college because you love one coach, who may already be job hunting behind the scenes, is the kind of thing you can point out by taking a longer, broader view. A lot can, and should, change for your student at this age. The right schools should be the right schools, for several reasons, so if one key criteria falls away, the list of prospective schools is still full of great options, not distant second-choice backups.

If your student has no idea what they might want to do for a career, or you don't really believe they are as set as they think they are, be sure you're looking at schools with excellent career offices. Many schools are really weak in this area, because parents and students don't think to consider this issue when choosing a school. Understandably the students are more focused on fabulous gyms or libraries or nice dorms that will impact their next four years. It's up to parents to do their homework on the schools to see how much career services is going to be able to do. Some schools have a strong career office but only regionally, which might be a plus or a minus, depending on your family's needs. Others might be very strong in graduate school placement, but not as strong in attracting big companies to campus to recruit students. If your student's interest is in the arts, where the jobs are more unique and the hunt will fall to the student, then you need a career team that provides a lot of great workshops and an alumni or parent network that can provide specific advice, even if they are unlikely to create internships or career positions for graduates.

Support Your Student Even if It Makes You Uncomfortable

Despite the fact that I'm pretty sure my message, addressed to students, is far more likely to be read by parents, I'm actually a huge advocate for landing your helicopter. I know how hard that can be—my husband, Mark, spent a good couple of years with the boys in high school quietly coaching me to "land the helicopter, put down the keys, and walk away." Prioritize where you push—if you drive them away through micromanagement, there's no career or family win to be had at any stage. For many students, freshman year requires unconditional love from home and nothing else. As worried as you may be about their eventual professional success, they just don't need a lot of help feeling bad. Some are getting a shock with their new grades, learning to live with their first roommate, breaking up with their first loves, making suboptimal nutrition and sleeping choices, and just living away from home. For some students this is a great time, but for most, there's always something a little surprising about the process. If nothing else, they've gone from the familiar to the new, and it's a shock to the system. Pushing freshman year may well need to be limited to getting them to go visit student health or the tutoring center. At this point, if they can solve all of their own problems without public parental intervention, it's a major new skill. Ask what you can do to help, and stalk the website so you can ask if they've been to the XYZ department in such and such a building. You can be helpful and supportive and let them develop the skills to manage their college lives, without adding to the new pressures they feel. Realistically most freshman are unlikely to have enough classes in their major to be a competitive candidate for an internship in the first place. From a career perspective, freshman summer is unlikely to result in a job offer no matter how successful the internship. You can just focus on taking the training wheels off, while perhaps silently running alongside the bike to provide a little emergency stability, and letting them delight in their new achievements.

Intervene directly only if you must. And if you do, even to the extent of bringing your student home mid-year to relaunch the next year, remember that they will eventually succeed if you provide supportive encouragement, but they may stop trying if you step in and take control of everything. Not only do they miss the chance to learn things about themselves and the world that way, but on an unspoken level that kind of intervention says that secretly you agree with their worst fears just as they feel they are failing—that they can't do it at all. Our job as parents may be to worry, sweat, and have our hearts broken for them with every disappointment, slight, or hurt they suffer, but not to spare them any of those opportunities to grow. Remember that they aren't great long-term planners, that they are still figuring out who they are, and that both of those facts have to result in failures. The goal is simply to fail forward—fail in such a way that they're able to make a better step forward next time as a result of the learning experience.

You should expect changes in plans; whether living arrangements, extra-curricular activities, majors, or even friends. They may not be telling you the whole story, but if they seem happy and healthy, you have to begin to let them to run their own lives. If there's compelling academic evidence that let you know the extracurriculars, whether purely social or incredibly worthy, are overshadowing the academics, then you may have to step back in. However many great, modern American fortunes have been made as a result of a student dropping out of college to start a business, most people who start college are going to be better off in the long run if they finish. It might be your money covering their tuition, and you may be able to convince them to take some business classes as a backup plan to being an art history major, but it's going to be a negotiation for most families to find a reasonable compromise. Based on my experience in the creative fields, most graphic designers, filmmakers, and writers do end up at least temporarily running their own one-person business, so some practical education in that area might nicely fill some elective space in their academic requirements. It may well be that the college they choose doesn't have anything that fits the bill, in which case perhaps the compromise is fitting in a summer community college or online class.

They may well fail at some things they try. If college admissions didn't teach your family this lesson, then sorority or fraternity rush may do so. There will be classes they don't get, auditions that don't result in a spot on the playbill, and internship and job interviews that don't result in offers. Expect that they may run for office and fail. There's never going to be any success if they don't try things and trying things involves failing at things. College is such a safe place to fail compared to the rest of life. As parents, much further down the path, it's easy to forget that failure in your twenties is not the same thing as it is later in life. College is a big enough place that failing isn't publicly embarrassing. There are dozens of other things to do instead, and there are always lots of other people interviewing, auditioning, running, trying out, and not succeeding. And having a backup plan for learning, making good use of the space a failure creates, can keep them in the game for a future win. Just as injured athletes sit on the bench, continuing to be with the team, and watch the games, a performer who doesn't land a performing role should take the chance to help the program by fundraising, learning lights, publicity, costumes, set design, or one of the other key positions required to create a successful show. When they are performing, knowing how to help a costume designer, lighting technician, or a producer succeed in their job will only make their big chance an even bigger success.

They may have completely crazy ideas about doing things you know they will never be able to afford or organize, but trying to figure out those projects and arriving at that conclusion on their own is to be hugely encouraged. Lots of people write bad business plans until they write a good one. Plenty of people write bad articles, stories, or screenplays, until they write a good one—or decide they aren't entrepreneurs or writers after all. But trying all those things can make them much better at the things they do end up doing. It gives them insights into useful processes and it develops real skills. The more times they present an idea and the more wide-ranging that audience, the more feedback they get about how to present. There are almost no careers in which presenting isn't valuable at some point. In most lives enthusiasm is always useful. Learning when to quit and move on to something new is a great skill to acquire and it's not one that any class will ever teach them, no matter how many times they earn an academic A.

Keep Your Eye on Post-graduation Life

You may have to push your student to get them into career services to start taking advantage of whatever services their school offers. As they get into their major and college life has solidified for them, it's likely you'll be the one most interested in ensuring they get off the family payroll. Get to know the school's website, or taking on some of the reading on careers, so you're in a good position to serve as an advisor might be really helpful for your student. The minute you start paving the path in a visible way, making calls to career services or lining up interviews, working on their résumé or LinkedIn profile, you've gone too far (no matter how busy your student is).

Fall of junior year is a great time for them to get going on informational interviews to get a feel for what skills they might need to be a strong candidate for an internship or career position. If your student is ready to make that effort and follow through quickly and effectively on any introductions you can make, then talk to them and explain the stakes. If they are ready—with a résumé, a LinkedIn account, and some genuine interest—then it's great to check in with your friends, colleagues, and neighbors about informational interviews. You're only going to get so many asks, so don't waste them if your student isn't ready to make the effort or just has no idea what might be interesting to them. Don't burn up a great connection by having your student blow it with a terrible impression too soon in the game. Even a simple failure to follow through by contacting the person in a timely manner is probably terminal for that avenue of exploration.

If career services can't help them with their career interests, then it's good to find that out now. See if there are any classes near their college that might be useful to them. You can reasonably do some background research in order to make proactive suggestions. Look for programs near home for the school breaks. Practical classes in career-specific software or other skills at university extensions or community colleges, are plentiful and reasonably priced. If your student is motivated, something as simple as an online subscription to a service like lynda.com can be sufficient for them to fill any technical skill gaps they may have.

If they just don't believe thinking about their post-college life is something they need to get going on, then you won't be able to convince them. As they begin to have graduating senior friends, they begin to realize the seniors who have to move home the day after graduation are not very happy at the prospect. Their peer group will help them come to this realization. Senior year will be full of stressed-out peers applying, interviewing, and hustling to line up a post-college plan. They will eventually get the idea.

Set Boundaries for Your Support

Support them financially, to the extent you are able. You can quite reasonably put requirements in place in exchange for tuition dollars. Requiring they live at home, maintain a given GPA, work a part-time job, or whatever else makes sense for your family is part of easing them into adult life. Our sons' colleges' merit aid awards both required a minimum 3.0 GPA. We didn't expect it to be an issue and it never was, but we used those requirements to state the family support was dependent on a 3.5 GPA. Our hope was to provide them room to experiment and try things they might not be great at, but not enough room to endanger their long-term prospects. During the years our sons were both in college, we emphasized taking advantage of opportunities in the summers more than acquiring minimum wage jobs. But those opportunities needed to either be in San Diego, so they could live at home while not being paid, or they needed to be funded in some fashion. I don't think it does students any good in becoming adults to have financial realities hidden. If you can't afford something or have financial concerns, college is a great time to talk about making affordable choices. Sensible money management is a key aspect of successful adulthood and it won't be covered in class or intuited by even the brightest students. Honest conversations about money, including how much help, if any, they can expect after graduation are essential to have with your student. Conversations about money when things are off to a good start will remove any perception of manipulation or punishment if you need to tighten the purse strings later because your student isn't making good use of their time in college.

Keep Doling Out More Responsibility

Once students enter the real world, they are going to need to book their own flights and get to places. Missing your connection going home for Thanksgiving freshman year or arriving back at school without your luggage is merely inconvenient, while missing the flight for the trade show or landing in Las Vegas without your suitcase while traveling in sweats with no ability to attack the problem is damaging to your career. In my years as a volunteer with our younger son's high school debate team I chaperoned dozens of the brightest, most ambitious teens at our excellent, nationally-ranked public high school. And every year we'd get to the big tournament at UC Berkeley and there would be some kids who couldn't get to the lobby of the hotel on time in the morning, making the whole group wait, risking missing first rounds as we raced to catch BART over to the campus, to get assignments for students and parent judges who then had to find the right classrooms on a very large, unfamiliar campus. The great thing about this experience was that the parent chaperones and the other teens would immediately tell the oversleeping students why this was unacceptable. The takeaway lesson for them was that their action had a direct consequence: other people were annoyed at being inconvenienced—at being forced to take on the additional emotional workload of being stressed out by someone else's mistakes. In this environment, their peers, the chaperones, and the coach would provide immediate negative feedback. And then we largely moved on. Maybe the next year in assigning rooms the chaperones would recall problems and think carefully about how the students were paired in the rooms.

In the real world, when you don't see that bigger picture and don't show up on time or fully prepared, the consequences are much bigger: your supervisor just doesn't trust you to get things done. Maybe they talk to you, maybe they send you to human resources, maybe they fire you, or maybe they just give you no real responsibilities for a while. There's no class or book that's going to give your student the list of the 550 things they need to be sure they never do. Despite the clickbait headlines on news sites that claim to tell people the 10 things their boss is thinking, or the 12 things new grads need to do to succeed, the information is just not out there in an easily digestible format. They've got to go out and fail when it doesn't matter. This is how they learn lessons that can be applied to other scenarios. And by seeing their peers in these same situations they learn those lessons, too. They need to mess up when the professionals around them are tolerant of errors and their peers are inexperienced enough to chew them out. That's the perfect life laboratory to conduct these experiments, even if accidentally.

It may seem obvious to some parents to point this out, but every time you wake your teen up to make sure they get to school on time today, you're preventing them from learning these lessons even more painlessly. Teach them to set their alarm the night before, buy them a louder alarm clock, or one that rolls away when it goes off. Do whatever you have to do, because getting up and out the door on time is a lesson that needs to be mastered before they leave for college. Otherwise you're potentially going to have paid for a very expensive semester with no academic credit when they miss too many class meetings to pass the class.

Support the College Community

Gone are the days when a few kids went off to college only to come home and join the family business. The odds that my kids want to come back and work for me or that yours will nicely follow your path into a similar career are pretty low. The best thing we can do for our own teens is to get involved and provide opportunities for each other's students. Even the best college career office has a finite network, but if each matriculating class also yields a couple of dozen parents willing to donate their time to speak to students about their own career, what they like or dislike about their job, where they think the industry is moving, the kinds of majors, minors, classes or work experiences that ended up being unexpectedly useful, the career office has a constantly renewing resource in its network. If you have a relationship with the career services office and a student comes along with an interest in something peripheral to your field, then perhaps you know someone else who might be willing to spend 30 minutes on the phone with that student in an informational interview.

If you work for a company that has many job openings for college students, connect your recruiting team with the college. Opening that door to create internships, even one-day externships or job shadowing opportunities can lead students to careers they would never have otherwise discovered. Students need to build out their world view of possibilities. They need to build out networks. Even your older children, who have already graduated, albeit from other schools, can be incredibly valuable for informational interviews. At the same time, encourage them to reach back to the schools from which they graduated. Giving back some of their time to support the school that educated them is a great way for them to build their presentation skills and grow their network. Transfer students shouldn't forget their original community college, either.

It's possible your student's school or one of the groups on campus runs programs in real-world transitions where you'd be a terrific speaker. Students need to learn how to make a budget, negotiate a salary, move to a new city, rent an apartment, or manage their credit. Most adults could successfully speak to these issues. Whatever your expertise, odds are a couple of hours of your time would be of huge value to someone else's student.

Talk to your child's friends, roommates, or teammates. They may never think to ask you what you do and how you got into it. Odds are it doesn't come up in their conversations when parents aren't around. Even the simple act of taking the conversational lead and starting those conversations helps them build the skills they need to reach out to other adults who are in the right fields. It's easy to forget that those young adults are still figuring out the world and their place in it. Aside from skill building and career interests, college can be hard for many reasons. Even more than in ordinary life, a kind word, a show of interest, an invitation to join your family for dinner, a walk, or a local Thanksgiving meal when a student can't get home, could mean the world to someone feeling a little overwhelmed by college life.

All schools need money well above and beyond what they collect in tuition, and if your student is on far more of a scholarship than your family needs, consider donating some of the money back. While colleges look for philanthropists and foundations to build libraries and stadiums, they also look for support within the community. Even if you're cutting back in order to cover college expenses, consider a very small donation. Larger donors are attracted to institutions and departments that can show a high percentage of participation within their student, parent, and alumni populations, so even a consistent $10 a year can have value that you might otherwise dismiss.

Most admissions departments are looking for alumni and parents outside their geographic area who can help recruit students.

By talking about your student's school with other families you can help generate interest in it, which enhances the school's reputation. Colleges and universities have magazines, newspapers, social media feeds, and apps. Find out about these and subscribe—they are likely to be free. The more you learn about your student's environment, the better equipped you are to see ways in which you can guide your student to resources they may need. Even if your student isn't an economics major, knowing about recent awards when you meet another family who has that interest can be very helpful.

Just as you can keep the big picture view in mind when your student is selecting a college, being up on departments, events, presentations, and other things on a campus far from home will let you provide useful guidance when asked. When your student is talking about changing their major, you might have some good ideas on things they haven't considered. When they don't get one of the newspaper writing slots, you can point out that you remember reading about the prize the campus science journal won last fall. Just as you would with a friend, you can make helpful suggestions with a basis in fact. It's up to your student to go investigate the feasibility of the suggestion and make their own decisions.

There's a lot parents can do to support a student in launching their life, but for the success to continue beyond that point, it is really important that the student do the heavy lifting. When they are lost you can provide directions, but don't drop everything to provide a ride. You can offer advice, but not dictate terms or majors. You can tell the truth about family resources, and suggest the impact those facts should have on their plans, but you can no longer give or withhold permission. You have to turn them loose into the world, and sometimes let the chips fall where they may. You have to use these four years to move from being any kind of an authority figure into becoming a trusted friend and advisor. At some point, after years of planning and lots of practice runs, the ground control staff just has hold their collective breath and wait to see if all the systems come together as indicated and the rocket launches successfully.

WHAT CAN COLLEGES DO?

In Fareed Zakaria's *In Defense of a Liberal Education,* he beautifully aligns the goals of a liberal arts education with some of the overall skills needed to succeed professionally throughout life. I think for both of our sons and many of their friends, college works exactly as it should. I see students blossom over the course of their college years and make many of the social and practical jumps they need to succeed. I think colleges are doing their best to link students with internships and first jobs.

Students simply don't know what they don't know. They take internships, accomplish all the tasks assigned, but cannot, for the most part, really pick up all the things they can. An internship is not like an academic course. A class provides a syllabus with clear-cut tasks in a coherent, expected, and unchanging order. There's a defined road map to success. Few workplaces can be that concrete in their expectations, and even those that have explicit guidelines are run by people—people who have their own opinions and observations. Perhaps you do everything on the list perfectly, but don't dress quite right, or speak up at meetings, or take on anything extra—without evidence that you can do a little extra, you may be slow to get promoted and paid to do a little extra. Most people don't go to work and just tackle their to-do list in a given day. Phones ring, emails chime, computers crash, and priorities shift very quickly. If a professor let herself run a class with shifting priorities, a survey of American history from 1776 to 1976 might not ever get out of the 1800s by the end of the semester.

The only place students can get a sense of the chaos that makes adult working life interesting and engaging is through their extracurricular involvements. There's a plethora of evidence as to how many students are spending their time on the party path through college, but if their social gains can be made at least in part while serving the college and larger community, they stand to gain far more than friendships. Those friendships, centered around meaningful pursuits, are likely to be deeper as well. While college athletes get a lot of practice working together as a team and planning for many contingencies on the field, they also get a lot of concierge service with professionals planning their workouts, ordering their uniforms, and making all their travel arrangements. That's a level of assistance they won't find in their careers for many years to come. With the growing trend toward reporting outcome metrics that include earnings, having students get their first job and also get promoted quickly may be a criteria colleges find heavily weighted in their rankings in the future. Even if such information and rankings aren't mandatory, success in these arenas can be publicized, perhaps helping both admissions and development offices.

This means colleges have to consider these outcomes. While many schools have been able to skate with substandard four- and five-year graduation rates, counting on unsophisticated consumers to overlook those warning signs, businesses will not be so forgiving with outcomes publicized. Schools with metrics showing successful grads will find more recruiters knocking on their doors, wanting to access this talent pool. And those with poor outcomes will quickly find that recruiters will catch on. Success will beget greater success where weakness will speed the rate of decay.

Experiment

In Rory Sutherland's TED Talk, "Sweat the Small Stuff," he implores organizations to consider a Chief Detail Officer. I've reproduced his grid on the next page, but the essence of his plea is that we spend too much time and money on a lot of things that might be better solved by focusing more thought on the small details that have a big impact. He calls for more experimenting with small changes in the user interface to address his fourth, unnamed quadrant for low-cost, high-impact efforts. I'm going to call it Insider Insight for my purposes. Colleges could conduct a review with a board of recent alumni a few years into the workforce who are empowered to look for those tweaks that cost little and might have a big effect. This demographic is still close enough to being a student at your school to know your programs, to see opportunities they enjoyed or missed, and to see how those helped or didn't in their first job or two. Ask your seniors and your on-campus recruiters what's resonating—the things that are valuable may be right in front of you and you've just got to expand access or help students highlight skills they already have. Every school is different, yet many likely have programs that could serve the need with a small amount of adjustment or expanded access. Ask your students' parents, too. In many cases, it's likely we need our helicopter tracking beams pried off our own children, and a good way to help us (and our students) is to get us involved helping other students. At the very least, getting working parents to talk from the perspective of being employers is a gold mine of information, much of which is easily accessed, and all of which is totally free.

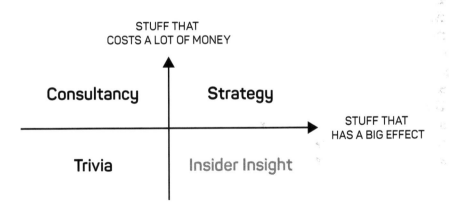

Systematize Engagement with the Career Process

The attitude about career offices on most campuses is "if we build it they will come" with the onus on students and their families to ensure that career exploration and preparation is happening. Colleges should have a series of checkpoints, starting in orientation, that require engagement with career services. Simply by making sure every freshman enters career services and has a LinkedIn profile, a college culture would change significantly. While these may not be graduation requirements, they should be in the category of vaccination records. These don't require massive budget increases. Upperclassmen in communications should be running one-hour seminars in LinkedIn profiles for freshmen. Film students can be running interviews, both to improve their documentary skills and show sophomores how they appear when interviewing. Staff can step in only to review the interview and give guidance for improvement or to run an interview preparation workshop. Parents and alumni can provide casual career panel forums when they are on campus for a weekend or for orientation. (What a great way to help pry those clingy freshmen parents away from their own children for an hour or two during move-in days, while engaging them in the larger community).

Support Campus Extracurriculars with Training

Students pursue an extraordinary number of extracurricular offices and memberships. They start in middle and high school, some out of true passion, others to check a box when they apply to college. Some come to college confident they are leaders, but less aware how much support there has been by parents, volunteers, teachers, and administrators.

Armed with confidence, and perhaps some public speaking skill, they run and win offices in college, too. Make those offices on your campus really mean something on their résumés. Make sure students who have been president of something have a working understanding of Robert's Rules of Order, that they know how to prepare agendas for meetings, and how to follow up on action items. If I interview a student who says they ran Delta Gamma Monday night meetings but can't elaborate, we're at a conversational dead end and I have to question the value of everything else on their résumé. But if "tell me about this" yields a conversation along the lines of "my college puts all new presidents and vice presidents through a four-hour training that makes sure we know how to prepare an agenda, have working knowledge of Robert's Rules of Order, delegate action items, and ensure our two annual formals and four annual fundraisers for the local animal shelter are successful", now I'm pretty impressed with the student—and the school.

On the back end, career services should be making sure the seniors with leadership on their résumés can hit the talking points persuasively. If I talk to two presidents at the same school while recruiting, I should be hearing pretty much the same thing. A variation of media training for your juniors and seniors so they stay on the university messaging should be part of every college's marketing budget. They are the most visible product out there on the ground, so make sure they are hitting the high points of your reputation. Ensure they can pitch a liberal arts education against a pre-professional major or vice-versa, depending what your school offers. Make sure their pitch for their school as they graduate aligns with what your admissions materials are saying to prospects.

Group secretary officers should be taught how to actually take minutes. Increasingly, I see adults slipping out smart phones with recording apps for minute taking. No one wants to wade through hours of recording or the resulting transcripts to discover a board voted to expand the fundraiser from three hours to four and the budget for next year was approved. Students serving as treasurer for their groups could be given basic instruction in spreadsheets and formatting financials. Have a committee review and develop a template for all campus organizations to use going forward. Ideally, it should be run by several juniors majoring in economics or business, who have already served a term as a successful treasurer, not a professor or administrator. Selecting the students should involve an interview and submission of their work as a treasurer—a great way to have a little ongoing quality control during the year as well as ensuring that treasurers know their work might be checked later when they apply for other campus gigs.

In my experience working on the board of a nonprofit staffed purely by volunteers, our technology teams across five chapters in San Diego found it hugely useful to meet two to three times a year to ponder our problems and solutions—most of the time someone else had created an elegant workaround for any problem a chapter reported. Our problems were rarely technology-based. They always lay in the human interaction with the technology. It was not only useful, but we all made friends we might not otherwise have made. Real life suffers from segregation across community differences as small as the age and sex of your children. It would typically be as unusual for me, as the mother of two sons in college, to have a 7th grade female soccer player's mom as a co-volunteer as it would be for a freshman lacrosse player to have a co-volunteer on campus from the International Student Association. And yet, it's obvious that having a more diverse set of inputs would be bound to improve the work.

And with athletes, maybe a little less concierge service. I know they are ridiculously busy. But out here in the real world, we adults are working hard at our jobs, raising families, getting pets to the vet, grocery shopping, and trying to exercise and sleep. As an undergraduate, I went to one of the PAC 12 schools—those football players had a very real full-time job. But they aren't busier than the average working professional with two kids—or busier than their peers who are also working a job while going to college. A little extra time explaining the team budget or having some team-related responsibilities can only be a good thing. Statistically we know most of them aren't going pro after graduation, and those who do would be well-advised to understand the real-world economics of budgets. I'm sure there are other tasks they can take on within the context of their sport, but if not, then I know plenty of coaches require the team do résumés, attend alumni interview night, or volunteer at a fundraiser. It's easy enough to also add that they take an active role in another group on campus, preferably one not already full of a majority of their teammates.

Students are always invited to pitch the student activity board if they have an idea for a club that doesn't exist, but once again, not everyone feels that passionately, or really believes that this is an open door. And some of those student boards are very insular and less open to new ideas. Some of the brightest and highest achieving students may be nearly crippled by parent micromanagement (See Julie Lithcott-Haims' excellent *How to Raise an Adult*). Some may still be tiger-parented into believing that some extracurriculars are worthless. Make sure this process is well publicized. Go overboard with encouragement for submissions. Preparatory workshops would provide time for them to come up with an idea and learn how to propose it. Maybe they know how much they'd get out of it, but can't tackle it on their own—then match them up. Some may just be wary of specific tasks: "A budget? I can't do that." That's why entrepreneurs find cofounders. If college is a lab for the students, then matchmaking or providing venues for matches to organically occur is well within their mission. Make sure your associated student council has an equitable and transparent scoring rubric for allocating funds.

Offer Leadership Workshops

While many students have impressive leadership résumés as they start college, in a best-case scenario they all have different skills and come from environments that award leadership for different reasons. For these students to begin to successfully take on college leadership roles requires some re-syncing with the new community's values and priorities. Corporations run training programs both to benefit their new staff and to maximize the speed and quality of the contributions those new hires will make to their organization. A unique program at Denison University, D.U. Lead, is an early fall weekend program open via application to a few first-year students. While the program hits a number of key leadership development notes for the chosen students, it also creates mentor roles for upperclassmen to nurture incoming leaders. That kind of program requires a limited amount of money and time and lends itself to being student-led in subsequent years.

Add a Required Orientation for All Students

Orientation programs serve both the long-term goals of successfully launching your graduates and also more successfully launches the new students into college. A network within school makes for a stronger community, while a more supportive culture improves freshman retention rates.

In our travels with both sons, we visited a representative sample of small liberal arts colleges, and although many had orientation programs, they varied in length, some had extra fees, and many were optional. None came anywhere near the stellar program offered by the University of Puget Sound. It's a student-run, award-winning, nine-day orientation for each set of incoming students. Students move in, parents are increasingly diverted to talks directed to them while the students begin to adjust to campus life. At the time our oldest son was going through this program, I remember being impressed at the gentle but unrelenting effort to pry my hands off my baby. In 2012 this consisted of moving Nick into the dorms while we were still in the hotel for another couple of days and concluded with a late-night Saturday trip to a local big box store via chartered buses for students only—forcing parents to say good-bye, since our activities were done. The schedule cleverly had the students arrive back at campus in the early hours of Sunday morning, while the next day started off in regular hours with student-only activities. The rest of orientation, which has no additional fee, has three parts: Prelude, Passages, and Perspectives. Prelude is another couple of days on campus with all students working with advisors, getting classes, getting used to dorms, the cafeteria, and other regular aspects of life. Then the new students are split into two groups, along the school colors of maroon and white. One group takes off for Passages, making the most of the Olympic Peninsula with camping, hiking, canoeing, or hanging out at base camp. The other set of students stays on campus for Perspectives, which revolves around campus activities and service groups in the Tacoma area—designed to get students acclimated to the college community as well as the larger city around them, all of which is navigated via Washington's strong public transit system. Puget Sound attracts a set of students skewed heavily towards service, the outdoors, and celebration of diversity. Probably not unlike many small liberal arts schools, and certainly those in the Pacific Northwest, but with the unique effort to integrate the students into the community environment on so many levels. All of it led is led by experienced students who plan, manage, lead, perform, and help the newcomers meet their own cohort. By the end there are very few students who don't feel they have a new home after seeing so many groups they might like to engage with during their time as students. I think everything about this program is designed to launch students perfectly, and more colleges should be developing orientation programs of this caliber.

Support New Students

While the living-learning experience of residential college is incredibly valuable, it is biased towards extroverts. There's no doubt an outgoing student makes a lot of connections with their peers. But the more introverted are going to have a harder time. Anticipate this: team freshmen and new transfers with experienced students. There's no doubt the athletic teams do this, if only accidentally.

Baseball players room with baseball players, while football and soccer teams are on campus earlier than everyone else to get started on their pre-season practices. When my son, Jake, arrived at Denison for the optional outdoor orientation, and moved into his dorm, I noticed many athletes were already on the all-male floor and rooming together. For a shy student this could have been disastrous. Surrounded by already-formed friendships that continue to lock down due to the large number of hours they spend together, shyer students can feel really intimidated.

All that information admissions has collected needs to be deployed through the summer—not just to match up roommates, but to create opportunities for the like-minded to find each other. By providing a group of potential English majors or recreational runners with a sophomore or junior who can function as a tour guide—introducing the students to relevant professors, showing them the best place for pizza or frozen yogurt—students who might be feeling shy, lonely, or overwhelmed get repeated chances to make friends and get swept up in events on campus. Make sure the mentor or buddy has enough information to help the student build on their high school extracurriculars to find college opportunities.

The mentors will build strong networking skills and get used to managing groups and making introductions, while the new students get exposed to the way your community actually works and a model of how adults interact. Everything in work is about being part of a larger group. While your head is down grinding out your to-do list, successful professionals are also trying to see the bigger picture and ensure they fit into that picture. Make use of a professor or administrator on campus who has good networking skills to help mentor the mentor/buddies. Think outside the box—perhaps someone in development at a small liberal arts college would be great at this, and deeper knowledge of students and groups on campus will make them stronger in speaking with alumni, parents, and other potential donors. In a large research university, there can be a lot of talent hidden away in departments that have nothing to do with students—don't let that go to waste. Post volunteer opportunities and bring interested employees into the fold—it can only increase their skills and improve staff retention.

Increase and Promote Opportunities for Tribes to Mix

In my experience, all companies have skilled professionals interacting across departmental barriers. As every campus seems to have a ton of students interested in marketing, advertising, or public relations, I have no idea why any college or university ever needs to have an ugly poster or flier for a campus event posted. And yet I saw them on every campus I visited with my sons. The art shows tended to have good-looking posters, of course, but the debate or mock trial teams didn't. This is evidence of a massive failure to connect different students. It seems like a simple, old-fashioned physical job board hosted by ASB or in the library would suffice for under $100 in expenses. Given the talents in colleges, I think there's an opportunity for someone to make an app and license it to schools, or for school to challenge their computer science students to interview stakeholders and develop real skills designing specs based on human needs, not just programming possibilities. Aspiring marketers and designers can be linked up with other student groups that would like to make use of their skills. Give them some basic ground rules on deadlines and payments. I know my son, Nick, sometimes needed posters for group event advertising and the student council would handle payments to the designer he hired—Maddie, a next-door neighbor from freshman year in the dorms on the humanities minor floor. That's a great example of two smart students networking in real-world fashion, so that's the outcome to promote. Colleges need to make it easier for accidental meetings and ad hoc working committees to happen.

Use the Breaks for Life Skills and Technical Certifications

When we looked at colleges, I was impressed that Macalester College had all their premed club students getting Wilderness First Responder certification in a January class. I have no idea if medical schools care or respond to this, but I think it's a smart, inexpensive way for the students to get some practical training in medicine as well as a few clinic hours long before they are applying to medical school. And I'm certain as a bonus, that other students and the larger Macalester community can only be safer with so many students knowing more than basic first aid. While any student can find these programs run by the National Outdoor Leadership School and work around their schedule, schools can remove the luck of random connections for all their students. They can subsidize the program financially, and provide enough students to get a program scheduled in dates that work perfectly for their academic breaks. Some schools run Habitat for Humanities or similar service trips during their extended January break. Some schools do run short workshops, but the vast majority of schools do nothing with the long winter break. In an era when parents are frequently both working outside the home, the ability of families to make constructive use of this long break is extremely limited. The reality is students go home and do nothing very useful with their time. They get home too late in the holiday shopping cycle to get short-term jobs to make extra cash, and they don't need that much time to catch up on sleep, dentist appointments, or visiting with friends. And they will never have vacations like that in the American working world, so thinking that much recovery time is normal or needed creates a bad cultural expectation as well.

Extensive, established winter terms or "J-terms" (one to three week January classes), like the programs run by Eckerd College in Florida, are few and far between. As I check their website for the 2016 postings, the pull quotes call out that their winter term offered a total of 15 countries to explore. Classes run about three weeks and they all have varying costs, although they note scholarships are available. The layout initially groups them by what requirements they fulfill. CIEE Study Abroad also runs three-and-half week January terms abroad, but at a $3,000 price point before airfare, they may not be feasible for many student budgets.

Colleges could very inexpensively make use of their three-week January breaks at relatively small additional cost by opening up the dorms and cafeteria early and bringing back a small quantity of faculty to run special intensives in their fields of interest. Grinnell College in Iowa offers a fascinating set of tutorials for their new students as part of their graduation requirements. The titles include Psychology of Humor; Comrades in the Kitchen: Russian Food and Culture in the Soviet Century; Icelandic Sagas; and Changing Childhoods. Perhaps that model of letting the professors teach a class focused on a passion might work for something shorter-term and outside the usual majors and minors—a broad overview with limited large as-signments, but a chance to bring other skills to bear.

A liberal arts college isn't likely to offer an accounting class, and even a school with a thriving undergraduate business major isn't going to easily attract humanities students for a whole semester of finance. Non-faculty could team up to cover a variety of sub-jects. Career services at most schools should easily be able to run a week's worth of intensive prep for internship and job hunting, which would be a much more useful schedule for athletes or performers, who might have a heavy practice or rehearsal schedule during the academic calendar's regular offerings. And while the protests of the expense are quite real, it's worth noting that every college and university routinely brings their athletes back to campus early, and many with a large international population have developed systems for keeping the dorms open through the shorter breaks for students who can't get home.

Formalize Succession Planning

While it's great that colleges let student organizations run them-selves, many newer organizations don't know how to hand off re-sponsibilities. Colleges should play the role of matchmaker, perhaps connecting new groups that have only a year or two under their belt with those that have survived several rounds of leadership gradua-tion. Talking about legacies, handing off leadership roles, exploring the reasons behind annual events, rather than the rote continuation of hollow traditions, could all enable new groups to survive and perhaps help older groups question some of their practices. Many colleges wrestle with hazing and have limited insight into both au-thorized and underground fraternities and sororities. Mandating short fall workshops focused on helping upperclassmen plan to train rising leaders to take over would enable that much-needed influence.

One of the constant struggles for business leaders during my time as a member with Young Entrepreneurs Organization and Women Presidents Organization was to work *on* their businesses in-stead of *in* their businesses. The idea is that all the time you spend actually doing the work of the business, being billable or saving on an external vendor cost by doing it yourself, the less time you have to work strategically on growing the business. In creative fields there's a double whammy here, because many managers loved their creative work and are sorry not to be actively generating ideas for specific clients. Designers go into the field because they like to design, but as they rise up the ranks, someday they find themselves managing other designers, and no longer actually doing the work they love. If you're mired in running the events for a club, you can hardly focus on the longer-term future for the organization. While some college presidents or deans might teach a random class to keep their hand in, most are freed from teaching for exactly these reasons. The college leadership should inevitably be full of workers who gave it up to be managers and leaders, so there's no question that gaining these skills, or even gaining the skills to evaluate whether you would want to make that move, would be incredibly useful for students in their post-college life.

Help Low-connectors Make Connections

Certainly every college provides an ample set of extracurricular options. And the extroverts and passionate fans will find their way to the right groups for them on campus. Colleges recognize that some of their students need writing or biology tutors, and some schools have great programs to meet the needs of their students who are the first in their families to attend college. Recognize the needs of low-connector students. Supply avenues to give them the little extra boosts they may need to succeed, by adding more on-ramps to orient them towards groups. This can be as simple as a skills or talent database, so groups looking for a treasurer or a graphic designer can come looking and find someone who hasn't had the nerve to put themselves out there.

Solicit Staff Involvement in Every Possible Way

Students will learn about navigating organizational structures, developing professional relationships, and accessing new opportunities only by repeatedly experiencing that process as they navigate the school's systems. The registrar and financial aid staff should see themselves in this light, not only helping the student with their immediate issue, but also helping them see the larger picture. I'm sure there are registrar offices that behave like government clerks, issuing edicts with no helpful information, and others that behave like the most well-meaning helicopter parents, taking over and solving the immediate problem. Perhaps the very same people behave both ways, depending on how they are asked for help. These non-academics should have some training in being teachers, in finding a middle way, like the best of all coworkers, who may not be able to help you right then, but can refer you to the right person—or like the best of all parents, who tells you how to change a tire and then hands over the tools so you can do it for yourself.

Utilize Parents and Alumni

Utilize parents and alumni to their fullest. Collect information on parent skills and professions and actively reach out to them asking if they are willing to do informational interviews when on campus to visit their student. Offer informal talks that any professional can lead if the subjects relate to their work experience. Create panels on career paths in the arts, first jobs, work disasters and lessons learned, things I'd tell my younger self to learn earlier, lucky breaks in my career, or how I found a mentor or a mentee. Parents and alumni who engage earlier and more often with students other than their own are also more likely to be receptive when the development office comes asking for a donation. Too frequently, the parent's first direct contact with a school comes right after the first tuition bill gets paid and involves another request for funds. Parents in less obviously affluent zip codes may receive no direct outreach at all.

With so many colleges actively recruiting international and first-generation students, parents and alumni can provide unique, much-needed, and powerful advice to students who are new to professional cultures in America. The world is changing quickly, and college students are doing all their learning in an environment that hasn't undergone substantial changes, except perhaps in information technology and mental health. Inviting visitors from the professional front lines to talk about their organizations, their needs now, and what they think the future might hold, can only benefit all college students. It may inspire some students to investigate professions they hadn't known existed, solidify current goals for others, and help them begin to build real networks that lead to successful long-term outcomes. Successful alumni are the ones most likely to give their time and money back to the school that helped provide their own launching pads, so it can only serve to create a virtuous cycle for the college itself.

When I talk to individual students about marketing and film careers, there is always a lot I don't know—my experience is very specific to the industries and geographies where our work is focused. I have only my own personal network to rely on when I want to connect a student with someone else. There's no insight into other parents or alumni who might be helpful.

There's also no direct way for me to connect with the students interested in all the possible career paths that might lead to self-employment. For those students, I have a lot of very specific, actionable advice (what a shock).

Colleges need to have a talent and speaker wish list and circulate that list within the larger college community. Every adult on campus has siblings, spouses, parents, college friends—all of whom might hold the answer for a particular student's specific question. An answer they'd willingly give, if asked. It has to fall on colleges to find a way to bridge these gaps and make those connections.

Implicitly Teach the Big Picture Process

Professors need support to fight back against the "will this be on the test?" mentality. Frank Bruni's *Where You Go Is Not Who You'll Be* has a terrifying chapter, "Strangled with Ivy", where he writes about his experience teaching at Princeton. He discusses his experience with other professors who posit the idea that students merely excel at getting *into* things, like Princeton or a visiting professor's class, but aren't good at continuing to mine those options for more opportunities. This is exactly why we see very bright students with bachelor's degrees who are mystified by their failure to get hired, or, if hired, to thrive in the next few years. Professors can fight this on their own only to some small degree. Colleges need to think about this in the context of the classes they offer. Maybe a freshman seminar dedicated more to the learning process than the result, much like freshman writing seminars, would meet that need. Changing existing classes doesn't have to increase faculty expenses. Shifting to more group projects, peer editing and peer grading don't require more faculty.

I don't think colleges should be giving credit for a life skills class—at some point the parents have to bear the brunt of these issues. But perhaps there is a middle ground, centered around a professor's expertise or a passion project class that centers around the group process. It could even be team taught—an engineering and art professor leading a class in making go-karts, for instance, or a history and economics professor getting small groups to plan how they might overthrow the administration (How to Plan a Revolution), a dance or music professor teaching with a communications professor on how to put on a show at the end of the semester. Modeling a less siloed approach to learning and working is key.

Any of these ideas lend themselves to the kinds of things I've suggested students organize and run, so don't be afraid to put students in charge of executing these ideas. Encountering obstacles, failing, and trying again with a different approach are far more important than a neat succession of academic successes.

SOURCES

Armstrong, Elizabeth & Hamilton, Laura. (2013). Paying for the Party: How College Maintains Inequality. Boston, MA. Harvard.

Arum, Richard & Roksa, Josipa. (2014). Aspiring Adults Adrift. Chicago, IL. University of Chicago Press.

Belkin, Douglas, "Test Finds College Graduates Lack Skills for White-Collar Jobs", The Wall Street Journal, January 16, 2015. http://www.wsj.com/articles/test-finds-many-students-ill-prepared-to-enter-work-force-1421432744

Bruni, Frank. (2015). Where You'll Go Is Not Who You'll Be. New York, NY. Grand Central Publishing.

Chambliss, Daniel F. & Takacs, Christopher G. (2014). How College Works. Boston, MA. Harvard.

Cronon, William, "Only Connect: The Goals of a Liberal Education", The American Scholar, Vol 67, No 4, Autumn 1998 https://sociology.stanford.edu/sites/default/files/publications/the_strength_of_weak_ties_and_exch_w-gans.pdf

Deresiewicz, William. (2014). Excellent Sheep: The Miseducation of the American Elite & the Way to a Meaningful Life. New York, NY. Simon & Schuster.

Fischer, Karin, "A College Degree Sorts Job Applicants, but Employers Wish It Meant More" The Chronicle of Higher Education, March 4, 2013 http://www.chronicle.com/article/The-Employment-Mismatch/137625/

Granovetter, Mark S., The Strength of Weak Ties (1973), American Journal of Sociology, Volume 78, Issue 6 (May, 1973), 1360-1380. https://sociology.stanford.edu/sites/default/files/publications/the_strength_of_weak_ties_and_exch_w-gans.pdf

Hoffman, R. and Casnocha, B. (2012). The Start-up of You. Crown Religion/Business/Forum

Howard, Jeff S., "Student Retention and First-Year Programs: A Comparison of Students in Liberal Arts Colleges in the Mountain South" (2013). Electronic Theses and Dissertations. Paper 2270. http://dc.etsu.edu/etd/2270

Jay, Meg. (2013). The Defining Decade: Why Your Twenties Matter—and How to Make the Most of Them. New York, NY. Grand Central Publishing.

Lythcott-Haims, Julie. (2015). How to Raise an Adult—Break Free of the Overparenting Trap and Prepare Your Kid for Success. New York, NY. Holt, Henry & Company, Inc.

National Association of Colleges and Employers, Job Outlook Report 2014

Roberts, Andrew. (2010). The Thinking Student's Guide to College: 75 Tips for Getting a Better Education. Chicago, IL. University of Chicago Press.

Rossi, A. (Producer, Director). (2014). The Ivory Tower [Motion Picture]. United States: CNN Films

Sandberg, S. (2010, December). Sheryl Sandberg: Why we have too few women leaders [video file]. Retrieved from: http://www.ted.com/talks/sheryl_sandberg_why_we_have_too_few_women_leaders

Sandberg, Sheryl. (2013). Lean In. New York, NY. Knopf Doubleday Publishing Group.

Scott, Amy, "What do employers really want from college grads?" American Public Media's Marketplace (Marketplace.org), March 1, 2013. http://www.marketplace.org/2013/03/01/education/what-do-employers-really-want-college-grads

St. Louis Community College Workforce Solutions Group, Report to the Region 2016

Sutherland, R. (2010, April). Rory Sutherland: Sweat the Small Stuff [video file]. Retrieved from: https://www.ted.com/talks/rory_sutherland_sweat_the_small_stuff

White, Martha C, "The Real Reason New College Grads Can't Get Hired", Time Magazine, November 10, 2013. http://business.time.com/2013/11/10/the-real-reason-new-college-grads-cant-get-hired/

Zakaria, Fareed. (2015). In Defense of a Liberal Education. Norton, W.W. & Company, Inc.

THE BASICS

MAKING A PROFESSIONAL IMPRESSION

I really believe most students know these fundamentals. However, the more people I discussed *Launch Like a Rocket* with as I was writing, the more requests I got for a section on the basics. This appendix is my effort to placate the professionals telling me there was a need for someone to say these things while not insulting all of you who already accept these as givens. Still, after a few years of tumbling out of bed in sweats and running off to class, it might be worth a quick review before you become a regular interviewee.

If your response to any of these is that you or someone in your office does these things and it's fine, my reply is simply "Who is actually saying it is fine?" Because my contention is no one is going to discuss these problems at all, but that these kinds of mistakes put a target on your back. Committing these subtle errors means your internship will not involve client contact, long-term mentorship, or a job offer. They mean your first job will not last long—that the contract will not be renewed, you will not be promoted, and when lay-offs are necessary, you will be first to go. Unless someone in HR is explicitly telling you flip-flops are part of the dress code, don't believe it. The inevitable organizational structure is a pyramid—don't get stuck in the lower levels because you fit in so well there.

Think About Every Detail—Is Anything a Reason to Reject You?

Assume you are being judged by a narrow-minded social conservative from 1950. There's a lot more leeway with art schools and creative jobs, but even in those fields, employers want to know you're willing to learn their systems and creative preferences (and their clients aren't always so wild) so you still need to be somewhat respectable. If you're from a place like San Diego, your sensibilities may be skewed too casual, so beware of that mistake. Reconsider the tattoo you want or at least the visible positioning of the potential tattoo. Yes, you're an adult, it's your body and your money. Your parents are super conservative or totally fine with it. On the other hand, the last thing you want just starting out is to be the brilliant young designer that no one takes to meetings. You don't know what you're missing out learning—but it's all the stuff you need to ultimately be creative director or strike out on your own. Already have the tattoo? Wear clothes that cover it, if possible, for the first couple of weeks, so people get to know you first. I'm not saying the bias is right, just saying it's there, and you won't get a chance to argue about it.

Shave, get a haircut, trim, wear a little makeup—whatever seems appropriate. Like choosing interview attire, you want to appear to fit in for a fairly middle-of-the-road take. People have more unconscious biases than they know. Your job, meeting several people during an interview, is to trigger all the biases in your favor, and none of the ones that aren't.

Consider Your Online persona

Use a library computer and Google yourself. Do a search within any social media you use. Do an image search. Make sure what a stranger sees is giving the right impression consistently. It's not enough to avoid too much skin and information showing online. If you are interviewing to be a junior account manager why does your account profile say you are a photographer? Don't hide who you are, but just be sure it all tells the story you want it to tell. Perhaps you'll be a better account manager because you are a passionate *amateur* photographer, but no employer wants to be the backup job. Don't let a potential interviewer become confused about your goals in life.

Check Your Handshake

Is it too limp, too crushing for a petite woman? Try it with professors, parents, neighbors—any professional who will give you honest feedback. Again, you might get hired, but you'll never get introduced to clients.

Confirm Your Résumé is Perfect

I know yours can't possibly have a mistake and yet about 50 percent of the résumés I see from people of all ages have a typo. I've seen bad email addresses, called phone numbers that don't work, seen mastery of misspelled software specified. How good can you be at all the nuances of Adobe Photoshop if you never noticed there's not a capital S in the middle?

Consider Your Email Address

I'm sure the college has given you one, but some people might prefer their personal email. It helps with first impressions if it's not soccergrrrl2020@yahoo.com but rather BrianneJones123@gmail.com. And watch the college-given emails. Colleges commonly take those away within a year of graduation and move you to an alumni-oriented one, so if you're job hunting senior year, I'd switch to an email you know won't change. You could be the runner-up for a position, and a perfect second job could fall in your lap a year later. Of course, the employer should check your very accurate LinkedIn profile to find you, but make it easy for them.

Look at People When They Are Talking to You

Never look at your phone in conversation, a meeting, or during a meal. Looking at your phone when anyone is speaking is a way of saying "You are boring and unimportant. I have better things to do." If that's something you would comfortably say out loud in that moment, then go ahead and look at your phone. Still can't judge? Okay, if at that moment it would be socially normal for someone to pick up a novel, open it, and start reading, then it's fine to look at your phone. Even as you rise up the ladder or if you're the client in the meeting, it's still out of bounds. If you really are expecting a call you'll have to take, then say so at the outset. If you start a meeting by setting the stage for a good reason why you'll have to take a call or a text and it really is an excellent reason, you'll be able to get away with it. For example, "I'm so sorry, but my dog is at the vet having surgery this morning, so I am going to keep an eye on my phone in case the vet calls during our meeting, so I can then step outside to take the call." would be fine in most cases.

Don't Eat Lunch Alone and Don't Do the Minimum

Make friends, ask questions, or just work so hard you miss lunch. You are trying to launch a career, so don't clock in and out like it's a factory gig.

While we're talking about clocking in and out: Be the first person in the office at least two days a week and the last one out another two days a week. Ideally vary this schedule or do more. You want to impress people, so you need to do a lot more than the minimum. If you're being paid hourly, check to see if it's okay—tell your boss you'd like to stay another hour to finish this draft, clean out the files, make another comp of the brochure—"would that be okay?" And if there's legitimately not anything for you to do, ask how else you can help. It is much better to make suggestions for things you see than to just blankly wait for a suggestion. We had an intern spontaneously go through a giant box of cords one year and re-coil and tie them all neatly—I still miss her in the office, a decade later. It takes so little to be the best intern ever. Really.

Dress Just a Little Better than the Job Requires

Look at people 1–2 steps above you and dress like them. Look at your peers and dress a little nicer. No professional job in an office will find flip-flops, exposed underwear (male or female, partial or full), cleavage (front or back), or an overbearing smell (Old Spice, perfume, or body odor) acceptable. Even a great smell shouldn't overtake the next workstation. I'm a huge fan of Banana Republic for first job clothing. Not too pricey but nice trousers, skirts, shirts, sweaters, jackets, and belts. Still, too pricey for you? Look at their website and then go duplicate the look. You don't have to be super cutting-edge. Everyone knows you are poor, even if you work in fashion, and they will cut you some slack. By the way, I'm all for a little friendly stalking to get this right before you interview—drive by, hang out in the lobby, get a feel for how people dress. The financial district is really different in cultural norms from high-tech and a university is very different than a hospital on that same university campus, or a business down the street.

Hollywood loves to show professional women in very high heels and very short skirts. And they love to dress actors up in clothes that are super trendy and expensive, then plunk them in office settings, as though this was normal. Real professionals don't dress that way. Sex sells TV ratings and movie tickets, not careers. Don't go broke buying your working wardrobe—very few work environments care all that much about expensive designer clothing and accessories. You want coworkers thinking about your talent, work ethic, and reliability, not wondering if you're single.

Send Thank You Emails and Stay in Touch

Most people send thank you emails for interviews, some do for informational interviews, but very few send thank yous for everything else. If you don't get the job, thank them for the notice and consider asking how you could have been a stronger candidate. Let them know where you land when you do get a new job. The world is increasingly a small town, everyone seems to have a few degrees of separation from someone else you know. You might have been the runner-up, so one more great impression might land you an unsolicited offer down the road.

Own Your Mistakes

Never make an *excuse* for an error. Apologies should be as pure as the driven snow—don't dilute yours by explaining the potentially really good reason why or how it happened. That's an excuse, not an apology. Own the error, express regret, offer a solution if possible. Apologize, fix it as you are able, ask what you need to ask to ensure it never happens again, and then promise that it will never happen again. Then deliver on your promise.

For example, if you oversleep and show up late, simply say you are so sorry and it won't happen again. Do not explain your flat tire, broken alarm, forgotten time change, or bad roommate, unless an explanation is specifically requested.

It's not the mistake, it's the unreliability that's the problem. You are hired to make other people's jobs easier, to independently handle as much of the work as you can. But if people can't consistently (100 percent) trust your work product's quality, thoroughness, and commitment, then there's no way they can give you a full workload, which means you aren't actually doing the job they hired you to do. An excuse establishes that you think the error was justified, a thought process that cements your unreliability. A solid apology can preserve your reputation for reliability. After a mistake that's the most urgent thing in need of repair.

Keep Improving

However great you are in any position, think about how you can be better. If you can't execute the work at a higher level, perhaps because it is super low-level work, think about how your process could be better. Ask how you could be better and more useful. Keep learning outside the office, and keep thinking about how what you see and hear can be applied to your career. While you're staying in touch with people you meet, continuing to ask for advice is a great reason to have coffee. Ask big picture questions: What do you wish you'd experienced earlier in your career? What were the key discoveries you made early in your career that led you to where you are now? Where do you think the big opportunities will be in 10 years? The more people you talk to who are in places you'd like to be, the better shot you have at being in the right place (on their mind) at the right time.